CONTENTS

EMPIRE
UNLEASHED
Your Entrepreneurial Roadmap
to Prosperity

DISCOVERING YOUR ENTREPRENEURIAL POTENTIAL

Grasping the Concept of Entrepreneurship
Entrepreneurship, with its aura of creativity, risk-taking, and limitless opportunity, is both an art and a science—a journey fraught with problems and successes. Understanding the essence of entrepreneurship requires delving into the very fabric of human inventiveness, resilience, and the unwavering pursuit of development.

At its foundation, entrepreneurship goes beyond the act of creating a business. It represents an attitude, a way of perceiving the world not as it is but as it could be. It is about seeing gaps, imagining solutions, and having the audacity to make ideas a reality. In "Empire Unleashed: Your Entrepreneurial Roadmap to Prosperity," we go on a journey to learn the complexities of entrepreneurship and embrace its revolutionary power.

Understanding the Entrepreneur's Mindset

Entrepreneurship starts with a mindset—an insatiable desire for invention combined with a determination to brave the unknown waters of uncertainty. It is about daring to question the status quo, disrupt industries, and forge new paths where none previously existed. The entrepreneurial mindset is characterized by persistence in the face of adversity, a voracious thirst for knowledge, and an unyielding trust in one's vision.

Accepting Risk and Failure

Acceptance of risk and the inevitability of failure are essential components of the entrepreneurial path. Entrepreneurship is not for the faint of heart; it takes guts to step into the unknown, risking one's resources and reputation in pursuit of a dream. However, failure teaches the most profound lessons, transforming individuals into seasoned entrepreneurs capable of weathering storms and capitalizing on chances in the face of uncertainty.

The Power of Innovation

Entrepreneurship is built around innovation, which drives progress and reshapes sectors.

Entrepreneurs use the power of innovation to address real problems, enhance people's lives, and push the boundaries of what is possible, whether through technological breakthroughs, creative business models, or disruptive ideas. In today's quickly changing market, innovation is more than just a competitive advantage; it is a requirement for existence.

Creating sustainable ventures

Beyond the appeal of rapid profits and sudden success, there is an imperative to create long-term value through sustainable initiatives. True entrepreneurship is more than just producing riches for oneself; it is also about fostering prosperity for society as a whole. It comprises creating enterprises that have a purpose, improve people's lives, and leave a beneficial impact on the world. Entrepreneurs who prioritize sustainability create opportunities for long-term growth, resilience, and meaningful influence.

Fostering an Ecosystem of Entrepreneurship

Entrepreneurship thrives in ecosystems that encourage collaboration, mentoring, and the free exchange of ideas. It is fostered by supportive communities, strong infrastructure, and favorable regulatory frameworks that allow prospective entrepreneurs to thrive. By creating an inclusive entrepreneurial ecosystem, we can unleash the full potential of human creativity, generate economic growth, and stimulate global social progress.

In "Empire Unleashed: Your Entrepreneurial Roadmap to Prosperity," we take readers on a transformative voyage of discovery, providing prospective entrepreneurs with the knowledge, insights, and skills they need to manage the intricacies of the entrepreneurial landscape. As we solve the mysteries of business, we discover not just the keys to riches but also the limitless potential that exists within each of us. So, let us go on this journey together, harnessing the force of entrepreneurship to create a brighter, more prosperous future for future generations.

The Fundamentals of Entrepreneurship
In the broad tapestry of business, entrepreneurship is the bold brushstroke that paints the picture of invention, resilience, and prosperity. Welcome to the first chapter of 'Empire Unleashed: Your Entrepreneurial Roadmap to Prosperity.' Here, we'll take a look at the fundamental concepts that govern the entrepreneurial spirit, unlocking the doors to success and paving the road for empire-building.

- The Entrepreneur's Mindset

Every successful entrepreneur has a distinct attitude, defined by a unique combination of desire, ingenuity, and a willingness to take risks. Cultivating an entrepreneurial mindset entails developing a strong sense of curiosity, adaptability, and a never-ending search for opportunity. Entrepreneurs regard problems as stepping stones rather than roadblocks, understanding that adversity frequently conceals the seeds of innovation.

- Vision and Mission

Entrepreneurship is more than just beginning a firm; it is about creating an idea, a vision that goes beyond the ordinary and motivates people toward their goals. Crafting a compelling vision and mission statement acts as a compass for entrepreneurs navigating the turbulent waters of the commercial world. This section discusses the significance of establishing clear objectives, developing a road map, and aligning every action with the overarching purpose that drives the entrepreneurial journey.

- Identifying opportunities

Successful entrepreneurs have an intuitive capacity to spot opportunities where others see obstacles. They have a deep understanding of market trends, consumer wants, and holes that need to be filled. This section goes into the skill of identifying opportunities, whether in developing technologies, undiscovered markets, or new solutions to current problems. Through case studies and real-world examples, we look at how entrepreneurs use their insights to create a competitive advantage.

- Risk management and resilience.

Entrepreneurship is naturally linked to risk, and mastering the skill of risk management is a must for success. This section discusses the numerous types of hazards that entrepreneurs face, ranging from financial and market dangers to personal and psychological problems. It discusses ways of avoiding these risks and fostering resilience—the ability to recover from setbacks stronger and more determined than before.

- Establishing a Strong Foundation

A strong foundation is essential for any sustainable empire. This section discusses the practical aspects of starting and running a firm, including legal issues, financial preparation, and operational tactics. Entrepreneurs learn about the core aspects that provide their businesses with stability and longevity, from choosing the correct business structure to analyzing financial statements.

- Innovation and Adaptability

In the dynamic world of entrepreneurship, innovation is the lifeblood that keeps businesses going through change. This section looks at how important it is to develop an innovative and adaptable culture within an entrepreneurial ecosystem. From embracing innovative technologies to pivoting business models, entrepreneurs learn how to manage the changing marketplace and stay ahead of the competition.

The Mentality of an Entrepreneur

Beginning the journey of entrepreneurship is more than just beginning a firm; it is a deep transformation in thinking. An entrepreneur's mindset is the compass that guides them through the turbulent waters of invention, risk, and the never-ending pursuit of achievement. In this chapter, we will go deeply into the psyche of the entrepreneur, examining the key aspects that form this distinct attitude.

Entrepreneurs have the ability to foresee a future that others may not perceive. This is known as visionary thinking. A visionary perspective allows them to recognize possibilities where others see challenges. They see problems as stepping stones to something better, rather than roadblocks. Entrepreneurs have a sharp sense of foresight in their pursuit of riches, constantly looking one step ahead.

Entrepreneurship requires a willingness to take risks and build resilience. Entrepreneurs recognize that taking calculated risks is necessary for growth and success. They accept uncertainty and see failure as a good learning opportunity rather than a defeat. Resilience becomes their armor, helping them to recover from failures with newfound determination. The ability to face and overcome hardship is a defining characteristic of the entrepreneurial spirit.

Entrepreneurs are lifelong learners who constantly seek to improve their knowledge and skills. They recognize that the business scene is constantly changing, and remaining relevant necessitates a commitment to continual education. Entrepreneurs cultivate a passion for information, whether through formal schooling, mentorship, or self-directed study, which feeds their ability to adapt and create in a quickly changing world.

Entrepreneurs prioritize adaptability. Adaptability is more than a virtue in today's fast-paced business world. Entrepreneurs are fast to pivot, alter their strategies, and welcome change. They realize that rigidity leads to obsolescence, whereas adaptation promotes resilience and maintains long-term viability in the face of changing market circumstances.

Entrepreneurs rely on their passion and perseverance to overcome problems. It is the fire that drives their creativity and determination. When combined with perseverance, passion becomes an effective catalyst for achievement. Entrepreneurs have an unrelenting devotion to their vision, and they are willing to weather storms and endure hardship in order to achieve their goals.

Entrepreneurs appreciate the importance of networking and teamwork for shared success. Building a strong network of mentors, peers, and industry contacts is a strategic need. They recognize that collaboration promotes creativity, offers varied perspectives, and creates new opportunities. The entrepreneurial mindset is based on the belief that success is often a collaborative endeavor.

Entrepreneurs are resourceful problem-solvers who see opportunities where others see constraints. Whether faced with financial limits or operational obstacles, they use their ingenuity and inventiveness to devise innovative solutions. The entrepreneurial mindset is based on the concept that restrictions are not obstacles but rather opportunities to think outside the box.

1. Having a purpose and passion
    Entrepreneurs are driven by passion to conquer challenges and persevere in the face of hardship. It is their steadfast faith in the importance of their concepts and the potential effects

they have. Conversely, purpose gives life direction and significance. It is the fundamental motivation behind entrepreneurs' actions, independent of financial benefit.

2. Originality and Ingenuity
Creative thinkers who question the status quo and think beyond the box are characteristics of entrepreneurs. They are always looking for fresh approaches to issues and satisfying demands from clients. Innovation is essential to entrepreneurship because it gives business owners a way to stand out from the crowd and establish a long-term competitive edge.

3. Taking Chances and Staying Strong
Embracing uncertainty and taking measured risks are essential components of entrepreneurship. Entrepreneurs see failure as a chance to develop and learn, acknowledging it as an inevitable part of the path. They are very resilient; they overcome adversity and turn it into a springboard for further achievement.

4. Flexibility and adaptability
Adaptability is essential for achieving success as an entrepreneur in the quickly evolving business environment

of today. When required, entrepreneurs must be prepared to adjust their tactics and welcome change. They are receptive to criticism and always looking for ways to get better.

5. Vision and Goal-Orientation Ambitious goals are made by entrepreneurs to direct their actions. They have a clear idea of what they want to accomplish. They are motivated to realize their mission and have a strong sense of purpose. They tirelessly pursue their objectives by breaking them down into manageable steps.

The Significance of Entrepreneurship

In the broad tapestry of economic and societal evolution, entrepreneurship serves as a cornerstone, a driving force that accelerates innovation, encourages economic progress, and shapes national destiny. "Empire Unleashed: Your Entrepreneurial Roadmap to Prosperity" takes readers on a trip to discover the tremendous significance of entrepreneurship in the modern world, highlighting its transformational potential and critical role in molding our collective future.

At its core, entrepreneurship is more than a business enterprise; it is a mindset, a spirit of adventure that embraces uncertainty and views setbacks as opportunities to improve. In a fast-changing global scene, entrepreneurs emerge as forward-thinking visionaries who dare to dream beyond the status quo and establish new paths.

One of the key qualities that distinguishes entrepreneurship is its ability to generate innovation. Entrepreneurs serve as catalysts for technical progress by pursuing unique ideas and developing groundbreaking solutions that push the boundaries of what is possible. In this never-ending drive for innovation, industries are changed, and the fundamental fabric of society undergoes profound transformations.

Furthermore, entrepreneurship is a major engine of economic growth. Entrepreneurs revitalize economies by launching new firms, encouraging competition, creating jobs, generating income, and contributing to community well-being. Successful entrepreneurial activities have far-reaching consequences, promoting a culture of economic resilience and long-term sustainability.

Entrepreneurship also plays a significant role in developing a culture of resilience and adaptation. In an era of extraordinary challenges, the capacity to navigate ambiguity and pivot in response to changing circumstances is a key characteristic of successful entrepreneurs. The lessons learned from both triumphs and losses serve as the foundation for personal and professional development, resulting in individuals who can weather storms and emerge stronger on the other side.

Furthermore, entrepreneurship can serve as a catalyst for societal change. Entrepreneurs who address unmet needs and push for creative solutions become positive change agents, defying cultural norms and contributing to the greater good. Whether through philanthropy, social enterprises, or lobbying, entrepreneurs are frequently at the vanguard of projects aimed at addressing serious social and environmental challenges and making a lasting impact on the global community.

"Empire Unleashed" acknowledges the link between entrepreneurship and empowerment. Entrepreneurial endeavors allow people to take control of their lives by providing a platform for self-expression and the pursuit of passions. Individuals may build their own narratives, redefine success on their own terms, and make important contributions to the world around them by using the lens of entrepreneurship.

The Ecosystem of Entrepreneurship
Entrepreneurship thrives in a supportive ecosystem; it is not an isolated endeavor. There are many different stakeholders in this ecosystem, such as governmental organizations, academic institutions, investors, mentors, and other business owners. These partners offer the networks, resources, and advice necessary for entrepreneurs to be successful.

Government programs and policies are essential for encouraging entrepreneurship. By lowering regulatory obstacles, opening up finance sources, and supporting entrepreneurship education, they can foster an atmosphere that is favorable to entrepreneurship. Academic establishments are equally essential in providing prospective business owners with the knowledge and abilities they need.

Entrepreneurs receive financial backing, knowledge, and direction from investors and mentors. They support business owners in honing their concepts, creating business strategies, and navigating the challenges of starting their own venture. A community of fellow entrepreneurs develops, providing companionship, teamwork, and insightful information.

In summary
The first step to realizing your entrepreneurial potential is to understand entrepreneurship. Through adopting an entrepreneurial attitude and developing the requisite abilities, you can begin off on a revolutionary path filled with creativity, expansion, and achievement. We'll look at finding your purpose and passion in the next section, as this will form the basis of your business ventures.

1.2 Determining Your Mission and Passion

Finding your passion and purpose is essential before starting an entrepreneurial adventure. Knowing your motivations and directing them toward your business endeavor will help you stay motivated and improve your chances of success. This section will help you build a solid foundation for your entrepreneurial journey by guiding you through the process of identifying your passion and purpose.

1.2.1 Examining Your Passions and Skills

Examining your hobbies and skills is the first step towards discovering your passion and purpose. Think back for a while about the things that make you happy and fulfilled. What activities do you like to do when you have free time? What qualities or abilities make you unique among others? You can begin to find possible business ideas that are in line with your passions by taking an inventory of your talents and interests.

1.2.2 Evaluating Individual Beliefs and Values

It's critical to evaluate your own values and beliefs in addition to investigating your hobbies and skills. What values do you uphold? Which fundamental beliefs guide you? Knowing your values will enable you to operate your company in a way that is consistent with your personal values, giving it meaning and fulfillment. For instance, you might want to think about launching a company that specializes in eco-friendly goods or services if you respect sustainability and environmental preservation.

1.2.3 Recognizing Issues and Finding Solutions

The goal of entrepreneurship is to satisfy client demands and solve difficulties. Think about the issues you are enthusiastic about resolving in order to determine your passion and mission. Which issues are you passionate about? What fixes are you able to offer for these issues? You can create a business that not only satisfies your passion but also has a beneficial social impact by concentrating on issues that you find personally meaningful.

1.2.4 Seeking Models of Inspiration

Finding your passion and purpose can be inspired and guided by looking up to successful businesspeople who have had a big influence. Investigate and discover the experiences of business owners who have established prosperous ventures in fields of interest to you. Recognize their goals, difficulties, and the influence they have had. You can learn how they matched their business endeavors with their passion and purpose by reading their biographies.

1.2.5 Trying and Testing Concepts

It's time to try out and evaluate your ideas once you have investigated your interests, evaluated your beliefs, recognized issues, and looked for inspiration. Begin by generating possible company concepts that are in line with your mission and areas of interest. Think about each idea's viability and demand in the market. Perform market research, get input from prospective clients, and hone your ideas. You can select the most viable company idea by reducing the number of possibilities you consider throughout this round of experimentation.

1.2.6 Fitting Purpose and Passion with Business Objectives

Making sure your passion and purpose line up with your business objectives is essential as you hone your business concept. Clearly state the difference you want to create and the principles you wish to follow in your mission and vision statements. From product creation to marketing techniques, every facet of your business should be infused with your passion and purpose. Your business objectives and your passion and purpose will work together to provide a solid foundation for long-term success.

1.2.7 Accepting Ongoing Education and Development

Finding your purpose and passion is a continuous journey rather than a one-time occurrence. As you advance in your entrepreneurial endeavors, never stop learning and developing. Continue to be inquisitive and receptive, looking for fresh chances to connect your mission and passion with your company. Accept criticism and modify your tactics as necessary. You can stay true to your passion and develop as an entrepreneur by always learning and developing.

1.2.8 Accepting Difficulties and Overcoming Roadblocks

Finding your passion and purpose is not always simple, and obstacles will unavoidably appear in your path. Accept these difficulties as chances for development and education. Resiliently and resolutely overcome challenges while remaining true to your goal and passion. Recall that becoming an entrepreneur is a journey, and obstacles are a normal part of the way. Through overcoming obstacles, you will strengthen your dedication to your passion and goals.

1.2.9 Accepting Your Path as an Entrepreneur

The first step in starting your own business is figuring out what your purpose and passion are. Welcome to this adventure with all of your energy and commitment. Keep your focus on your mission and passion, and let them lead you through the highs and lows of being an entrepreneur. Keep in mind that creating a great business requires time and work, but you can overcome challenges and leave a lasting impression if you have a clear sense of purpose.

Remember as you proceed that your mission and passion could change over time. Remain aware of your inner drives and remain receptive to fresh chances that fit your principles. You can build a profitable company and find pleasure and meaning in your entrepreneurial pursuits by discovering your passion and purpose.

1.3 Creating an Attitude of Entrepreneurship

Developing an entrepreneurial attitude is essential to being a successful entrepreneur. This way of thinking is the cornerstone around which your empire will be constructed. It's a method of problem-solving and thinking that will help you get through the erratic and always shifting corporate environment. Creating an entrepreneurial mindset means forming specific attitudes, convictions, and routines that will enable you to take chances, accept setbacks, and grasp opportunities. This section will examine the essential components of an entrepreneurial mentality and offer doable tactics for fostering and enhancing it.

1.3.1 Adopting a Growth Perspective

Adopting a growth mindset is one of the core components of an entrepreneurial attitude. The idea that skills and intelligence can be acquired through commitment, work, and a desire to study defines this way of thinking. When you have a growth mentality, failure is seen as a necessary step toward achievement, and obstacles are seen as chances for personal development. You are willing to change and grow, are receptive to criticism, and are a lifelong learner. In order to foster a growth mentality, one should:

Accept challenges: Seek out challenges on a proactive basis rather than dodging them. Difficulties present chances for development and learning. Accept them as an opportunity to grow and learn new abilities.

Accept failure: It's not the end; rather, it's a worthwhile educational experience. Accept failure as a chance to grow, change, and learn. Examine your mistakes, determine what you can learn from them, and apply those lessons to your next attempts.

Foster a passion for learning by becoming insatiably curious and always looking for new and exciting possibilities to learn and advance. Maintain your curiosity by reading books, going to lectures, enrolling in classes, and surrounding yourself with positive and challenging individuals.

Accept feedback. It's a great instrument for personal development. Ask peers, consumers, and mentors for their opinions. Remain receptive to constructive criticism and utilize it to hone your abilities and clarify your concepts.

1.3.2 Building Perseverance and Resilience

Being an entrepreneur is not an easy path. It is rife with challenges, disappointments, and periods of uncertainty. To get beyond these obstacles and keep going, one must have resilience and tenacity. Perseverance is the will to press on in the face of difficulties, whereas resilience is the capacity to recover from adversity. The following are some methods for building resilience and persistence:

Create a solid support network for yourself by surrounding yourself with mentors, advisors, and like-minded people who can offer direction, encouragement, and support when things get tough.

Take care of your physical and emotional health by engaging in self-care. Take part in things that will aid in your relaxation, recharging, and mental well-being. Exercise, meditation, spending quality time with loved ones, and engaging in hobbies are a few examples of this.

Have reasonable expectations. Recognize that being an entrepreneur is a journey with ups and downs. Be ready for setbacks and establish reasonable expectations. Accept setbacks as teaching moments and channel them into more drive for success.

Remind yourself of your long-term goals and the difference you wish to create in order to stay focused on your vision. This will support you in maintaining your commitment and motivation in the face of difficulties.

1.3.3 Fostering Innovation and Creativity

Thinking creatively and coming up with original solutions to issues are essential components of being an entrepreneur. It's crucial to foster originality and innovation if you want to stand out from the competition and provide your clients with something special. The following are some methods to encourage originality and creativity:

Accept curiosity: Continue to be inquisitive and ask questions. Examine alternatives and refute presumptions. Be receptive to many viewpoints and concepts.

Encourage your staff to exchange ideas and think creatively in order to cultivate an innovative culture. Establish a setting that rewards exploration and measured risk-taking.

Look for ideas from a variety of sources: Get involved in a variety of fields, professions, and cultures. Get ideas from a variety of places, such as literature, artwork, travel, and discussions with others from various backgrounds.

Accept failure as a teaching opportunity. Don't be afraid to try new things, and don't be afraid of failing. Take lessons from your mistakes and channel them into new ideas and inventive endeavors.

1.3.4 Building a Robust Work Ethic

Being an entrepreneur means having a strong work ethic, perseverance, and dedication. The key to reaching your objectives and creating a prosperous empire is cultivating a strong work ethic. The following are some methods to cultivate a solid work ethic:

Establish definite objectives: Establish your objectives and divide them into manageable steps. To make sure you are moving closer to your objectives, make a plan and rank your assignments.

Develop discipline: Make routines and follow them to help you stay disciplined. Remain focused on your priorities and steer clear of distractions.

Adopt a proactive mentality by using your initiative to look for possibilities and find solutions to issues. Make things happen instead of waiting for them to happen.

Practice time management: set priorities for your work, assign duties to others when needed, and refrain from putting things off.

Accept hard labor and the fact that success does not happen quickly. Accept hard work and be prepared to invest the time and energy needed to reach your objectives.

It takes time to cultivate an entrepreneurial attitude. It necessitates introspection, self-control, and a dedication to personal development. You may fully realize your business potential and create a successful empire by adopting a growth mentality, becoming resilient and persistent, encouraging creativity and innovation, and maintaining a strong work ethic.

1.4   Overcoming   Typical   Obstacles   in Entrepreneurship

Becoming an entrepreneur and launching a business are thrilling and fulfilling experiences. It is not without difficulties, though. We will examine some of the typical challenges faced by business owners in this part and offer solutions. You may improve your chances of success and create a prosperous empire by being aware of these obstacles and taking decisive action to overcome them.

1.4.1 Handling Risk and Uncertainty

Handling risk and uncertainty is one of the main problems faced by entrepreneurs. There are no assurances that a new venture will be successful, and it requires taking a risk. You can overcome these obstacles more skillfully, though, if you embrace ambiguity and take measured chances.

It is essential to perform in-depth market research and compile as much data as you can on your target market, rivals, and industry trends in order to handle uncertainty. This will assist you in making well-informed choices and reduce the risks involved in launching a business.

Creating a backup plan might also assist you in reducing possible dangers. Determine the main risks that your company might encounter and develop plans to mitigate them. Having a backup plan in place can help you deal with unforeseen obstacles more skillfully and lessen their negative effects on your company.

1.4.2 Getting Rid of the Failure Fear

One of the biggest problems that many entrepreneurs have is the fear of failing. It can be crippling to be afraid of failing, keeping you from taking the required chances to expand your company. But it's crucial to keep in mind that failing is a normal aspect of becoming an entrepreneur.

You must change your perspective and see failure

as a chance for learning if you want to get over your fear of failing. Adopt a growth mentality and recognize that each obstacle presents a chance for development. Continue forward motion, modify your tactics, and accept lessons from your past blunders.

You can also get over your fear of failing by surrounding yourself with a network of like-minded people, mentors, and other entrepreneurs. Seek advice and assistance from those who have gone through comparable struggles, as they may offer insightful opinions and motivation.

1.4.3 Setting and enforcing priorities
As an entrepreneur, you will frequently have to juggle a variety of duties and wear many hats. Setting priorities for your work and managing your time well are essential for being productive and reaching your objectives.

Start by determining which of your chores are the most critical, then rank them in order of importance to conquer the time management difficulty. Concentrate on tasks that directly advance the expansion and prosperity of your company. Assign duties that are capable of being completed by others so that you can concentrate on high-value tasks.

Making the most of your time and remaining organized can also be achieved by putting good time management strategies into practice, such as making a timetable, establishing deadlines, and using productivity tools. Make sure you are efficiently allocating your time and resources by reviewing and reevaluating your priorities on a regular basis.

1.4.4 Creating a Robust Support Network

Being an entrepreneur can be a solitary path; therefore, maintaining motivation and conquering obstacles require a solid support network. Be in the company of people who share your goal and who can offer you direction, encouragement, and support.

Creating a network of fellow business owners, mentors, and advisers can yield insightful opinions. To meet others who share your interests, look for networking opportunities, join trade associations, and go to conferences and events. Talk about what's important to you, exchange stories, and get knowledge from those who have gone through similar struggles.

In order to network and exchange experiences with other entrepreneurs, you should also think about participating in online forums or entrepreneurial communities. These communities can offer a forum for asking for advice and comments, as well as a feeling of support and belonging.

Preserving work-life equilibrium
Because entrepreneurship frequently involves

hard work and dedication, it can be difficult to strike a healthy work-life balance. Neglecting your personal health, however, might result in burnout and have a detrimental effect on your company.

It's critical to create a schedule that balances work and leisure time in order to overcome this obstacle. Make self-care activities a priority, including rest, exercise, and quality time with loved ones. Assign work when it can be done and develop a sense of trust in your group to complete duties.

Developing a work environment that is encouraging and prioritizes work-life balance can also improve your general wellbeing. Lead by example and push your colleagues to put their personal lives first. Maintaining a good work-life balance can help you stay motivated, creative, and full of energy, all of which will be good for your company.

In summary
There are many hurdles on the path of becoming an entrepreneur, but with the right knowledge and preparation, you can conquer them and create a prosperous empire. Some of the most important tactics for surviving the entrepreneurial landscape are learning to live with uncertainty, conquering the fear of failing, setting and achieving goals, forming a solid support network, and preserving work-life balance. Accept these difficulties as chances for development and

education, and allow them to help you succeed as an entrepreneur.

FROM IDEA TO CONCEPT

2.1 Carrying Out Market Research
An essential first step in developing your business

idea into a profitable endeavor is market research. It entails obtaining and evaluating data regarding your intended audience, rivals, and market trends in order to make wise choices and confirm the feasibility of your idea. By carrying out in-depth market research, you can obtain insightful information that will direct your business plan and raise your chances of success.

2.1.1 Recognizing the Value of Market Research

You can gain a thorough grasp of your target market's requirements, preferences, and behaviors by conducting market research. It assists you in determining market trends, evaluating the level of demand for your good or service, and spotting new prospects and difficulties. You can decide on your business concept, positioning, pricing, and marketing methods by obtaining information and insights.

2.1.2 Clarifying Your Study Goals

Establishing your research objectives is crucial before you begin any market research. What particular details are you looking to collect? What are the objectives you expect to accomplish with your research? You can concentrate your efforts and make sure that you collect the most pertinent and helpful data by outlining your objectives explicitly.

2.1.3 Determining Your Ideal Clientele

Finding your target market is one of the first steps in conducting market research. Who are the perfect clients for you? What are the behaviors, interests, and demographics of this group? You may better adapt your product or service to your target market's demands and preferences by being aware of who they are. Surveys, interviews, and the analysis of current data can all be used to learn more about your target market.

2.1.4 Examining Rivals

Examining your rivals is yet another essential component of market research. Who are your rivals, both direct and indirect? What are their advantages and disadvantages? You can spot market gaps and figure out how to set your company apart by researching your rivals. Examine their offerings, costs, promotional plans, and client feedback to acquire knowledge that will assist you in properly positioning your company.

2.1.5 Data Collection

There are several ways to collect information for market research. Direct data collection from your target market through surveys, interviews, focus groups, or observations is known as primary research. Analyzing pre-existing data from sources including government publications, industry reports, and internet databases is known as secondary research. Primary and secondary research approaches are both beneficial and can offer you a variety of viewpoints and ideas.

2.1.6 Data Analysis and Interpretation

Effective analysis and interpretation of the data

are crucial after you have acquired the required information. Examine the data for correlations, trends, and patterns that might help you make business decisions. Utilize qualitative analytical approaches to extract insights from open-ended responses and statistical tools and procedures to assess quantitative data. You may find opportunities, validate your company idea, and make wise judgments by analyzing the data.

2.1.7 Verifying Your Business Concept

Conducting market research is essential to the validation of your business concept. You can determine the level of demand for your good or service, locate new clients, and comprehend their requirements and preferences by obtaining data and insights. By going through this validation process, you may improve your concept, make the required changes, and raise your company's chances of success when it launches.

2.1.8 Changing with the Market

Conducting market research is a continuous process. It's critical to keep an eye on market developments and adjust as your company grows. Keep abreast of market developments, consumer inclinations, and rival tactics. To stay ahead of the competition, do market research on a regular basis to find new prospects, evaluate the success of your marketing campaigns, and make well-informed decisions.

2.1.9 Using Technology to Conduct Market

Research

Technology has completely changed the manner in which market research is carried out. Data collection and analysis are made more effective by online surveys, social media listening tools, and data analytics systems, which also offer insightful information. Utilize these developments in technology to collect information, monitor consumer mood, and obtain a competitive advantage in the marketplace.

2.1.10: Having Conversations with Your Target Audience

Doing market research offers you the chance to interact with your target audience in addition to the traditional data collection process. Engaging prospective clients in the research process allows you to establish rapport, earn their confidence, and obtain insightful input. To gain a deeper understanding of your target market's needs, interests, and pain areas, interact with them through surveys, focus groups, or online forums.

2.1.11: Making Knowledgeable Business Choices

Market research provides you with valuable insights that enable you to make well-informed business decisions. When it comes to creating your product, pricing strategy, marketing plan, or expansion plan, market research gives you the information and understanding you need to make choices that suit the demands and preferences of your target market.

2.1.12 Verdict

An essential first step in developing your business idea into a profitable endeavor is market research. You may boost your chances of success, validate your concept, and make well-informed decisions by researching your target market, rivals, and industry. Conducting continuous market research enables you to interact with your target audience, adjust to shifting market conditions, and make wise business choices. Accept market research as a potent instrument to realize your full entrepreneurial potential and create a profitable empire.

2.2 Evaluating the Demand in the Market

Evaluating consumer demand is a critical first step in making your business idea a profitable endeavor. Finding out if there is a market for your product or service is crucial before devoting time, energy, and resources to further developing your concept. You can learn a lot about your target market, the competition, and possible profitability by evaluating market demand. This section will cover a variety of methods and approaches to assist you in accurately determining market demand.

2.2.1 Recognizing Your Desired Readership

You need a thorough understanding of your target market in order to make an accurate assessment of market demand. The people or organizations that are most likely to be interested in and buy your product or service make up your target audience. Through comprehension of their requirements, inclinations, and actions, you can customize your offering to fulfill their particular demands.

Consider doing market research to learn more about your target audience. Surveys, interviews, focus groups, and the analysis of current data can all be used for this. You can create a thorough profile of your target audience by learning about the psychographics, buying patterns, and demographics of your potential clients. Your sales and marketing plans will be built around this profile.

2.2.2 Examining Competition and Market Trends

Analyzing market trends and competition in depth is also necessary for determining demand. You can spot business prospects and potential obstacles by knowing the state of the market today. To learn more about the general market size, growth rate, and major trends, start by reading industry reports, market studies, and competition analyses.

Evaluating your rivals is just as crucial. Determine who your immediate and indirect rivals are, then assess their advantages, disadvantages, and placement in the market. You can use this study to find market gaps that your product or service can close. You can differentiate your offering and create a special value proposition by researching your competitors.

2.2.3 Holding Focus Groups and Surveys
Focus groups and surveys are useful instruments for determining market demand. By using surveys, you can get quantifiable information on a broad sample of respondents' requirements, preferences, and readiness to pay for your good or service. Focus groups, on the other hand, entail assembling a small group of people to participate in a discussion about your idea under guidance. This qualitative method enables a thorough investigation of viewpoints, driving forces, and potential adoption roadblocks.

Make sure that the questions you ask in focus groups and surveys are objective, straightforward, and succinct. For the purpose of gathering both quantitative and qualitative data, combine open-ended and closed-ended questions. To assure the quality and dependability of your data and to reach a larger audience, think about utilizing online survey platforms or hiring market research companies.

2.2.4 Testing the MVP, or Minimum Viable Product

Testing a Minimum Viable Product (MVP) is a useful method for determining the demand in the market. Before devoting substantial resources to development, you can obtain feedback and evaluate your concept with an MVP, which is a condensed version of your product or service. You can test the MVP with a small number of early adopters or beta testers to see how well it works, get their input, and make any necessary changes.

During the MVP testing process, closely observe user input and behavior. Examine willingness to pay, satisfaction levels, and usage trends. Based on customer preferences and demands, this data can help you fine-tune your offering and offer insightful information about the demand for your product or service.

2.2.5 Evaluating the Stability of Finances

Analyzing market demand also entails determining whether your business idea is financially feasible. Ascertain your concept's possible revenue streams, pricing policies, and cost structure. When estimating your profitability, take into account variables like overhead, marketing costs, and production costs.

Make sure you do a comprehensive financial analysis that includes a predicted income statement and a break-even analysis. You can use this research to determine whether your business idea can be sustained financially and whether there is enough market demand to meet your revenue targets. If the financial estimates show that your idea won't be profitable, think about improving it or looking into different company strategies.

2.2.6 Keeping an eye on consumer and industry trends

Since customer and industry trends are constantly changing, it is critical to keep an eye on market demand. Keep abreast of the most recent events, innovations in technology, and changes in customer tastes that could affect your company. You can proactively modify your offering to satisfy shifting market demands and keep a competitive edge by staying ahead of the curve.

Participate at conferences and trade exhibitions, read trade periodicals, and interact with your target market on social media and in online forums. By being involved in industry discussions and maintaining contact with your clients, you can spot new trends and modify your company plan appropriately.

In summary

Evaluating consumer demand is a crucial phase in the idea-to-empire process. You may learn a lot about the need for your product or service by knowing your target market, studying market trends and competitors, running focus groups and surveys, testing an MVP, assessing financial viability, and keeping an eye on consumer and industry developments. Equipped with this understanding, you may strategize your business for market success, improve your concept, and make well-informed judgments.

2.3 Assessing the Viability of Your Idea

It is critical to test the viability of your business idea after you have completed market research and evaluated the need for it. To find out if your proposal has the potential to be successful in the market, testing the viability of your idea entails trying it out, collecting feedback, and assessing the results. By going through this procedure, you can verify your hypotheses, find any weaknesses, and make the required corrections before devoting a substantial amount of time and money to your project.

2.3.1 Getting Input

Consult with industry experts, other

entrepreneurs, and potential customers to get their feedback on your idea's practicality. This input might give you insightful information and point out any holes or places where your notion needs work. Here are a few efficient methods for getting feedback:

Surveys and Questionnaires: To gain input from your intended audience, create online surveys or questionnaires. Inquire specifically about their requirements, inclinations, and viewpoints in relation to your business concept.

Focus Groups: Set up focus groups with people who match the demographics of your target market. Encourage dialogue to learn more about people's opinions, views, and expectations about your idea.

One-on-One Interviews: To better grasp the viewpoints of mentors, industry experts, and prospective consumers, do one-on-one interviews with them. Pose open-ended inquiries to elicit in-depth answers.

Testing your idea Using a Prototype: Create a Minimum Viable Product (MVP) to evaluate the usability and functionality of your idea. After users interact with your prototype, get their feedback to find out what works and what doesn't.

Social Media Listening: Keep an eye on online forums and social media sites to see what people are saying about comparable goods and services.

Talk to prospective clients and pay attention to their opinions.

2.3.2 Carrying out Research

Experiments can yield useful information to evaluate the viability of your business idea, in addition to providing feedback. With the use of experiments, you can test various facets of your idea and gauge how well it meets the needs of your target audience. These are some possible experiments for you to try:

Pilot Programs: To test your idea in a controlled setting, start a small-scale pilot program. This enables you to collect feedback and real-world facts from a small number of clients before expanding.

A/B testing: Make multiple iterations of your service, product, or marketing plan, then compare them to see which works best. This might assist you in tailoring your offering to the tastes of your customers.

Landing Page Testing: Create a landing page that highlights your offering and tracks the percentage of visitors that sign up or make a purchase. This can reveal information about the degree of demand and interest in your offering.

Price testing: Try out various pricing tactics to find the best price range for your good or service. This will assist you in comprehending how customers perceive prices and make decisions about what to buy.

Partnership Testing: To gauge how the market will react to your service, work with influencers or firms that complement each other. This might assist you in determining the likelihood of strategic alliances and collaborations.

2.3.3 Examining Information and Making Modifications

After conducting trials and gathering feedback, it's critical to examine the results and make well-informed changes to your business plan. You can improve your concept through this iterative approach by taking into account market feedback and real-world observations. The actions to take are as follows:

Analyze the information gathered from experiments, questionnaires, interviews, and other sources. Seek out important insights, patterns, and trends that can guide your decision-making.

Determine strengths and weaknesses: Using data analysis and feedback, determine the advantages and disadvantages of your business concept. Find out which parts of your idea are appealing to clients and which ones require work.

Make Modifications: Make the required changes to your concept using the knowledge you've received from the data analysis and feedback. This could entail changing your marketing approach, your target market, or the attributes of your product.

Test Once More: Put the modifications into practice and carry out additional testing to confirm the success of the modifications. Iterate on your idea and keep getting feedback until you have a workable, commercially viable solution.

You may improve your company's chances of success by performing trials, getting feedback, and evaluating data to test the viability of your idea. By going through this iterative process, you may improve your idea, fix any problems, and match your product to the requirements and tastes of your target market. To maintain the long-term viability and profitability of your organization, keep in mind that testing and validation are continuous procedures that should be continued throughout the business's lifecycle.

2.4 Honing and Extending Your Idea

It's time to hone and improve your concept

after you've verified the feasibility of your business idea and gotten input from prospective clients. This phase is essential for guaranteeing that your offering satisfies the requirements and inclinations of your intended consumer base. You may improve your concept's value proposition, set it apart from competitors, and raise the likelihood that it will succeed in the market by honing and improving it.

2.4.1 Examining Customer Feedback Carefully examining the input you obtained from testers is one of the first steps towards fine-tuning your idea. You can use focus groups, interviews, surveys, or any other technique you use to get information from prospective clients to provide this feedback. To find places where changes can be made, look for recurring themes and patterns in the feedback.

Take careful note of any problems or difficulties that clients bring up. These insights can assist you in finding ways to improve your offering and better meet the needs of your customers. Additionally, record any compliments or aspects that customers found especially appealing. These elements can be highlighted even further and used to set your notion apart from rivals' offerings.

2.4.2 Finding Opportunities for Development Determine which particular aspects of your concept need modification based on the examination of client input. Aspects including product attributes, cost, packaging, branding, and customer experience may fall under this category. Sort the categories according to importance for the entire value offer and deal with them in a methodical manner.

To validate your assumptions and obtain further insights, think about carrying out extra market research. You can gain a better understanding of consumer preferences, market trends, and competition dynamics by using this research. You may make wise choices regarding honing your notion and strategically placing it by keeping up with industry developments.

2.4.3 Improving the Proposition for Value
Improve the value proposition of your concept as you work to make it better. The special mix of advantages and value that your product or service provides to clients is known as the value proposition. It is what distinguishes you from rivals and persuades clients to select your product.

Think about how you may enhance your product or service's features, functionality, or performance to better satisfy the expectations of your clients. Seek methods to set your concept apart from the competition by filling a need in the market or by providing something that they don't. This could entail developing fresh approaches to provide value or enhancing already-existing features.

2.4.4 Testing and Iterating

Iteratively refining your concept entails testing modifications with your target market and making adjustments depending on input. Create a new version of your concept and include the improvements you found. This might be an improved marketing approach, a revamped company plan, or a prototype.

Once your concept has been revised, test it on a small sample of prospective clients. Get input on the modifications you made and evaluate if the enhancements have addressed the prior preferences and pain issues. If more iteration is required, make additional modifications in light of the input you have received.

2.4.5 Tracking and Assessing Achievement
It's critical to track and evaluate the progress of your concept as you make changes and revisions. Establish precise measurements and key performance indicators (KPIs) to monitor the effects of your modifications. Metrics like market share, client retention, revenue growth, and customer happiness may be included in this.

To ascertain whether your refinements are working, periodically go over the data and do an analysis of the findings. If the modifications have proved beneficial, keep improving them and look into new possibilities. If the outcomes do not meet your expectations, review your strategy and take other options into consideration.

2.4.6 Seeking Professional Guidance

Seeking professional counsel might be helpful during the complex process of refining and iterating your proposal. Think about speaking with mentors, business advisers, or industry experts who can offer insightful advice. Their knowledge and experience may guide you through obstacles, point out blind spots, and assist you in making wise choices.

Throughout the refining process, think about asking your target market for their input. Talk to prospective clients, hear what they have to say, and include them in the development of your idea. Your target audience may become more devoted and have a feeling of ownership as a result of this cooperative approach.

2.4.7 Notifying Stakeholders of Changes

It's critical to properly inform your stakeholders of the modifications as you hone and improve your concept. Customers, partners, investors, and team members are all included in this. Express your improvements and the value they add to the market in a clear and concise manner.

Make sure that everyone on your team is aware of the adjustments and how they will benefit the concept as a whole. Share the improvements with your partners and investors, emphasizing how they will increase the potential of the company. Lastly, let your clients know about the improvements and how they take their preferences and needs into account.

You may improve your concept's value proposition and raise the likelihood that it will succeed by modifying and reworking it in response to input from customers and industry analysis. Accept that this is an iterative process, and be willing to make adjustments as you learn more. Keep in mind that developing your concept is a lifelong process that calls for constant learning and modification.

CRAFTING A STRATEGIC BUSINESS PLAN

3.1 Establishing Your Goals and Vision

The guiding concepts that define and give direction to your company are its vision and mission. They act as the cornerstones around which your empire is constructed. This section will discuss the significance of clearly stating your vision and mission, as well as offer you doable strategies for crafting an engaging and significant statement.

3.1.1 Realizing the Significance of Mission and Vision

Your business plan's vision and mission statements are crucial parts. They inform internal and external stakeholders about your goals, values, and purpose. This is why they are essential:

Making Strategic Decisions: Your mission and vision statements serve as a compass, directing your choices and guaranteeing that they are in line with your long-term objectives.

Inspiring and motivating: A well-written vision and mission statement can instill a sense of togetherness and purpose in your workforce.

Differentiating Your Business: By emphasizing your distinctive value proposition and the effect you hope to achieve, your vision and mission statements help set your company apart from the competition.

Bringing in Clients and Investors: Investors who see your potential and customers who share your vision and goal can be drawn in by having a strong and engaging vision and mission statement.

3.1.2 Formulating Your Goal Proposition

Your vision statement is a succinct and motivational description of your long-term goals. It gives a clear picture of the direction you want to take your company. To create a compelling vision statement, adhere to these guidelines:

Consider Your Purpose: Let's begin by considering the motivation behind your initial foray into entrepreneurship. What issue are you trying to resolve? Which effect are you hoping to achieve? Make your view more shaped by these reflections.

Think about the future: Imagine your company in a few years, when it is at its peak. How does one define success? What changes have you seen in your business? Summarize this vision in a few phrases.

Be Clear and Inspiring: Your vision statement should inspire enthusiasm while being sufficiently clear to give direction. To express your goals, choose language that is strong and emotive.

Keep It Concise: Make your vision statement memorable and succinct. Steer clear of technical phrases and jargon that could offend or confuse your readers.

3.1.3 Formulating Your Goal Declaration

The goal of your company and the steps you plan to take to realize your vision are described in your mission statement. It should be a succinct and straightforward statement that conveys your main principles, your intended audience, and the benefits you offer. To create a mission statement that is effective, follow these steps:

Define Your Core Values: Determine the guiding principles of your company. These are the guiding concepts that influence your choices and behavior. Think about your priorities and the way you would like to run your firm.

Determine Who Your Target Market Is: Give your target market or clientele a precise definition. Who do they represent? What are their problems and needs? In what ways does your company meet those needs?

Express Your Worth Proposal: Identify the special value that your company provides to clients. What distinguishes you from your rivals? How can you better than anyone else satisfy their needs or solve their problems?

Create a clear and concise statement: Condense your target audience, value proposition, and fundamental beliefs into a mission statement that is both clear and succinct. Ensure that all internal and external stakeholders can understand it with ease.

3.1.4 Harmonizing Your Objective and Vision

It is imperative to guarantee congruence between your mission and vision statements after they have been formulated. The path to realizing your vision should be outlined in your mission statement. Here's how to successfully align them:

Examine your purpose and vision statements side by side to assess consistency. Make sure your mission statement clearly advances and aids in the accomplishment of your goal.

Verify Clarity: Ensure that your mission and vision statements are understandable and unambiguous. Steer clear of confusing or vague language since this could cause misunderstandings or confusion.

Get Input: Show your goal and vision statements to dependable team members, mentors, or advisers. Get input and, if needed, make changes. Several points of view are necessary to guarantee alignment and clarity.

Communicate Both Internally and Externally: After your vision and mission statements are complete, make sure you effectively share them with your staff, clients, and stakeholders. Make sure that everyone is aware of and supportive of the common goal and direction.

Keep in mind that your mission and vision statements are subject to change. You might need to go over and improve them again as your company grows in order to make sure they stay inspiring and relevant. Check their alignment with your values and goals on a regular basis, and adapt as necessary.

You lay the foundation for your entrepreneurial journey by establishing your vision and objectives. These declarations will direct your decision-making, motivate your group, and draw in clients and investors who are aligned with your mission. Accept the strength of a compelling goal and vision, and allow them to drive you as you establish your empire.

3.2 Making SMART Objectives

One of the most important steps in creating a strategic company plan is setting goals. It becomes challenging to monitor development and maintain focus on the path to success in the absence of specific, quantifiable goals. We'll look at the idea of SMART goals in this section and see how you may use it on your entrepreneurial path.

3.2.1 Comprehending SMART Objectives

The words "specific, measurable, achievable, relevant, and time-bound" are abbreviated as "SMART." With the help of this framework, you can develop goals in an organized manner and make sure they are specific and doable. Let's dissect each element of the SMART objectives:

Specific: Objectives must be precise, unambiguous, and succinct. To avoid having a general objective like "increase sales," a more targeted one would be "increase sales by 20% in the next quarter." You can concentrate your efforts and distribute resources wisely if you are specific.

Measurable: In order to monitor and assess progress, goals ought to be measurable. Measurable objectives give you a standard by which to evaluate your progress. A measurable aim can be, for instance, "increase customer satisfaction ratings from 80% to 90% within six months" rather than "improve customer satisfaction."

Achievable: Objectives must be reachable and reasonable. Setting lofty objectives is vital, but they should also be doable. Unrealistic goals can cause dissatisfaction and demotivation. When defining attainable goals, take into account your strengths, limitations, and available resources.

Relevant: Your goals ought to be in line with your mission and overarching vision. They ought to support your long-term performance and be pertinent to your company's goals. You risk wasting time and energy by setting goals that are not in line with your strategic direction and fundamental values.

Time-bound: Objectives ought to have a set amount of time to be accomplished. Establishing deadlines helps prioritize work and fosters a sense of urgency. To avoid having an open-ended objective like "launch a new product," one could have a time-bound goal like "launch a new product by the end of the second quarter."

3.2.2 The Value of SMART Goal-Setting
SMART goal-setting is crucial for a number of reasons:

Clarity and Focus: By outlining your objectives precisely, SMART goals help you stay focused and achieve your goals. They remove all doubt and guarantee that all parties are aware of the intended result.

Motivation and Accountability: By offering you a tangible objective to strive for, SMART goals boost your motivation. As you monitor and assess your accomplishments in relation to the predetermined goals, they also help you take responsibility for your development.

Resource Allocation: You can more efficiently allocate resources if you set SMART goals. By establishing objectives that are precise and quantifiable, you can determine the resources needed to reach them and distribute them appropriately.

Assessment and Enhancement: SMART objectives facilitate assessment and enhancement. By comparing your progress to the predetermined goals, you can find areas for growth and make the required corrections to keep moving forward.

3.2.3 Using SMART Objectives in Your Company

Now that you know how important SMART objectives are, let's look at how you can use them in your company:

Your goals should be in line with your overarching vision and mission, so start there. Think about how reaching these targets will help you realize your long-term goals.

Divide your objectives: Divide your long-term goals into smaller, more doable tasks. They will be simpler to monitor and accomplish as a result. Every goal ought to be clear, quantifiable, doable, pertinent, and time-bound.

Set priorities for your objectives: Establish the priorities for your goals and order them according to importance. Determine which objectives will have the most effects on your company and devote your resources appropriately.

Assign responsibility: Clearly state who is in charge of each objective, and make sure they have the tools and assistance they need to complete it. Assigning duties encourages accountability and guarantees that progress is being made.

Track development: Track and observe your goals' progress on a regular basis. Utilize key performance indicators (KPIs) to gauge accomplishment and pinpoint areas in need of development. To stay on course, make the appropriate modifications.

Celebrate your accomplishments and major turning points in your journey. Acknowledging and rewarding your team's accomplishments will keep them motivated and moving forward.

Recall that creating SMART goals is a continuous process. You might need to modify your goals as your company grows and situations change. Make sure your goals are still pertinent and in line with your overarching vision by reviewing and reevaluating them on a regular basis.

You will have a clear path to success and be more capable of handling the chances and obstacles that come your way if you develop SMART goals. Thus, give your goals some thought, make them smart, and realize the maximum potential of your entrepreneurial endeavors.

3.3 Examining the Market Environment

Knowing the competitive landscape in the dynamic world of business is essential to your venture's success. By examining the competitive environment, you can find out who your rivals are, learn a lot about your sector, and strategically place your company. You can find opportunities, reduce risks, and create winning tactics to set yourself apart from the competition by performing a thorough study. This section will go over the essential procedures and resources you may utilize to assess the competitive environment and obtain a competitive edge.

3.3.1 Recognizing Rivals

Finding your rivals is the first step in assessing the competitive environment. It's critical to take into account both direct and indirect competitors. While indirect competitors could provide different solutions or target a somewhat different clientele, direct competitors sell comparable goods and services to the same target market. You can begin by performing market research, looking through industry data, and examining consumer feedback to determine who your competitors are. You can also look for companies operating in your industry and region using online resources and platforms.

3.3.2 Evaluating the Advantages and Disadvantages of Rivals

The next step is to evaluate your competitors' strengths and shortcomings after you have recognized them. Gaining an understanding of your competitors' strong points and areas for improvement will help you make informed decisions about your own business plan. You can examine their web presence, price policies, marketing plans, client testimonials, and goods and services. You can learn from your competitors' successes and come up with unique strategies to set yourself apart by figuring out what makes them successful. In a similar vein, you may take advantage of such flaws to your advantage and provide your clients with an even better value proposition.

3.3.3 Assessing Positioning in the Market

The way your target market views your company in comparison to your rivals is known as market positioning. Assessing your market positioning is crucial if you want to know how to stand out from the competition and develop a special selling point. You can examine elements like product quality, pricing, customer service, customer perception, and brand reputation to assess your market positioning. You can decide how to distinguish yourself from the competition and draw in your target clientele by knowing where your company is in the market.

3.3.4 Performing a SWOT evaluation

A SWOT analysis is an effective tool that you may use to evaluate both your competitors and your own company. Strengths, weaknesses, opportunities, and threats are referred to as SWOT. You may determine the external opportunities and market threats, as well as the internal strengths and weaknesses of your company, by performing a SWOT analysis. This analysis can help you make decisions by giving you a thorough picture of your competitive environment. It can assist you in maximizing your advantages, addressing your shortcomings, taking advantage of opportunities, and averting dangers.

3.3.5 Keeping an eye on market trends

It is essential to keep an eye on market trends and stay current on new releases in order to stay one step ahead of the competition. Technological developments, alterations in customer behavior, modifications to regulations, and the emergence of new market opportunities are examples of industry trends. You may position yourself as an industry leader and adjust your business plan accordingly if you stay educated. Through market research, trade journals, conferences, trade exhibitions, and networking with other industry professionals, you can keep an eye on industry trends.

3.3.6 Examining Client Input

An invaluable resource for information when examining the competitive environment is customer feedback. You may learn about your clients' wants, preferences, and pain areas by paying attention to what they have to say. You can find possibilities to set yourself apart from the competition by analyzing client feedback to see where they might be lacking. Direct communication, social media monitoring, online reviews, questionnaires, and other methods can all be used to get client feedback. Gaining a competitive edge and cultivating a devoted clientele can be achieved by promptly attending to consumer grievances and consistently enhancing your offerings.

3.3.7 Comparison Shopping and Ongoing Enhancement

Benchmarking is the process of evaluating how well your company performs in relation to best practices and industry standards. You can find out where you are doing well and where you need to make improvements in your business by benchmarking it. Through this method, you can set reasonable goals for your own firm and learn from the top performers in your field. Constantly improving your business's performance through small, regular adjustments is known as continuous improvement. It is possible to remain ahead of the competition and satisfy the changing wants of your clientele by consistently enhancing your offerings, procedures, and services.

In conclusion, one of the most important steps in creating a winning business plan is assessing the competitive environment. You can gain valuable insights and develop effective strategies to gain a competitive advantage by identifying your competitors, analyzing their strengths and weaknesses, evaluating your market positioning, conducting a SWOT analysis, keeping an eye on industry trends, analyzing customer feedback, and benchmarking your business. Recall that the competitive environment is ever-changing; therefore, in order to stay ahead of the game, you must constantly assess and modify your approach.

3.4 Formulating a Plan for Marketing

The success of your firm depends on creating a solid marketing plan in the cutthroat business world of today. In addition to assisting you in reaching your target audience, a well-thought-out marketing plan will set your company apart from the competition and spur expansion. This section will cover the essential elements of a marketing strategy and offer helpful advice on how to create a workable plan.

3.4.1 Recognizing Your Ideal Customer

A thorough grasp of your target market is essential before you can create a marketing plan. This entails figuring out the requirements, tastes, and habits of your target clientele. You may learn a lot about your target market by acquiring customer insights and conducting market research.

Begin by drafting fictionalized descriptions of your ideal clientele, or buyer personas. Take into account variables like purchasing patterns, psychographics, and demography. This will allow you to customize your marketing so that it appeals to your target market.

Furthermore, examine your rivals' positioning and marketing tactics to gain insight into their business practices. Find the gaps and possibilities you may take advantage of to set your company apart from the competition and draw clients.

3.4.2 Outlining Your Special Value Offer
Identifying your unique value proposition (UVP) is a crucial step in creating a marketing plan. What distinguishes your company from rivals and conveys the value you provide to clients is your unique value proposition (UVP). It should make it very evident why clients ought to select your goods or services above rivals.

Think about the following inquiries when defining your UVP:

What issue does your offering help clients with?
What distinguishes your product or service from the competition?
How does your offering benefit and add value for consumers?
Create an engaging UVP that speaks to your target market and clearly conveys the advantages of

picking your company.

3.4.3 Selecting Appropriate Marketing Channels

It's time to select the best marketing channels to reach your audience after you have a firm grasp on your target market and distinctive value offer. Choosing the best online and offline marketing channels for your company is essential. There are many different types of marketing channels accessible.

Think about your target audience's traits and preferred methods of communication. For instance, digital marketing methods like social media platforms and email marketing might be more successful if your target audience is made up of young professionals. On the other hand, conventional marketing avenues like print media and direct mail might be more suitable if your target audience is older and less tech-aware.

Remember that a multi-channel strategy is frequently the most successful. You may expand your audience and improve your chances of success by combining offline and online marketing strategies.

3.4.4 Creating Marketing Messages That Are Powerful

Your marketing communications must be captivating if you want to draw in clients and properly convey your value proposition. Your target audience should be able to relate to your marketing messaging, which should be succinct and unambiguous.

Determine the main advantages and characteristics of your good or service first. Emphasize how these advantages solve the problems that your target audience is facing. Instead of using jargon or technical phrases that could alienate or confuse potential clients, utilize accessible and simple language.

Adapt your marketing communications to the various phases of the client journey. For instance, during the awareness stage, concentrate on building brand recognition and informing your target market about the issue that your good or service addresses. During the contemplation phase, emphasize the special qualities and advantages of your product. And to establish credibility and trust during the decision-making process, offer testimonies and social proof.

3.4.5 Choosing Metrics and Objectives for Marketing

It is crucial to establish specific objectives and KPIs in order to assess the success of your marketing campaigns. Your marketing objectives should be SMART (specific, measurable, achievable, relevant, and time-bound) and should be in line with your overarching business goals.

Increasing brand exposure, creating leads, boosting website traffic, and boosting revenue are a few typical marketing objectives. Choose the important metrics that will enable you to monitor your progress after you have established your objectives. These measurements could include things like conversion rates, social media interaction, website analytics, and client acquisition expenses.

Make data-driven decisions to maximize your efforts by tracking and analyzing your marketing analytics on a regular basis to assess the effectiveness of your marketing plan.

3.4.6 Putting Your Marketing Strategy into Practice and Assessing It
It's time to put your plan into action and carry out your marketing campaigns now that you have a clear marketing strategy in place. To effectively contact your target audience and convey your marketing messaging, make use of the marketing channels you have selected.

Keep an eye on the results of your marketing initiatives and assess their efficacy in relation to your objectives and performance indicators. To enhance your outcomes, make the appropriate modifications and improvements. Iterate and test your marketing methods often to determine which ones work best for your company.

Keep in mind that marketing is a continuous process that needs to be continuously monitored, assessed, and adjusted in order to stay ahead of the competition and promote corporate expansion.

Creating a thorough marketing plan that fits your target market and corporate goals can put you in a strong position to draw in new clients, stand out from the competition, and succeed in the long run.

3.5 Formulating a Budget

A strong financial strategy is the foundation of any profitable company. It offers a path for handling the financial aspects of your business, making sure you comprehend your sources of income, outlays, and profitability. Making well-informed decisions, allocating resources efficiently, and navigating future financial obstacles are all made possible by creating a financial plan. We will go over the essential elements of a financial plan in this part and walk you through the process of drafting one for your business.

3.5.1 Establishing Budgetary Objectives

Setting specific financial goals for your company is crucial before getting into the finer points of your financial plan. These objectives will act as standards by which to gauge the success and advancement of your business. Establish your short- and long-term financial goals first. While long-term objectives can include growing market share or reaching a particular return on investment, short-term objectives might include reaching a particular monthly revenue target or cutting costs.

Making sure your financial objectives are SMART —specific, measurable, achievable, relevant, and time-bound—is essential when setting them. You can set attainable and doable goals with the aid of this framework. Rather than establishing a general objective such as "increase revenue," a SMART goal would say, for instance, "increase monthly revenue by 10% within the next six months through targeted marketing campaigns and expanding into new markets."

3.5.2 Revenue Estimation

One of the most important parts of your financial plan is revenue estimation. It entails estimating how much revenue your company anticipates making from its goods and services over a given time frame. You must take into account a number of variables, including market demand, pricing strategy, competition, and sales channels, in order to effectively predict revenue.

Analyze your target market and determine the level of demand for your products or services first. To find new clients and learn about their preferences and readiness to pay, conduct market research. You can use this information to evaluate the potential money you can produce and to gauge the size of your target market.

Think about your pricing approach next. Based on

elements including perceived value, rival pricing, and production costs, decide on the best price point for your goods or services. Achieving a balance between optimizing revenue and maintaining market competitiveness is crucial.

Take into account the many sales channels that your company has at its disposal as well. Will you use an online store or a physical location to sell directly to consumers? Which party will you use—wholesalers or distributors? It is critical to assess each sales channel's possible impact on your overall revenue estimates because they may have varying revenue implications.

3.5.3 Managing Expenses and Budgeting

Two essential elements of any financial strategy are managing your spending and creating a budget. A clearly established budget aids in the efficient use of resources, cost containment, and guaranteeing that your company stays within its means. Begin by listing every expense related to operating your firm, including variable costs (raw materials, marketing charges) and fixed costs (rent, electricity, payroll).

Sort your spending into several cost centers, such as marketing, administration, and operations. You'll be able to keep better track of and control your spending as a result. To establish a comprehensive budget that includes estimated costs for each cost center, think about utilizing spreadsheets or budgeting software.

Review your budget on a regular basis and make sure it matches your real spending. This will assist you in finding any differences and making the required corrections. You can find areas where you can cut costs or reallocate resources to increase efficiency and profitability by keeping a careful eye on your expenditures.

3.5.4 Management of Cash Flow

Effective management of cash flow is essential to the financial well-being of your company. It entails keeping an eye on your cash input and outflow to make sure you have enough to cover your responsibilities. If your company's cash flow is positive, it means it is making more money than it is spending; if it is negative, the converse is true.

Making a cash flow projection is the first step towards managing your cash flow successfully. This forecast, which is usually made on a monthly or quarterly basis, projects the timing and volume of cash inflows and outflows over a given time period. It enables you to foresee possible cash surpluses or shortages and take proactive steps to deal with them.

Determine the main sources of income, such as investments, loans, and sales revenue. Take into account the time of these influxes as well as any possible lags or variations. Regarding costs, take into account when and how much should be paid for different bills, including rent, salary, and supplier bills.

You can spot possible cash flow gaps and take the necessary action by routinely monitoring your cash flow and comparing it to your projection. This could be extending credit terms to suppliers, tightening up credit control procedures, or looking into other financial sources to cover any gaps.

3.5.5 Analysis and Projections of Finance

A forward-looking perspective of your company's financial performance is offered by financial predictions. They support you in making wise judgments, luring in possible lenders or investors, and evaluating the viability and profitability of your endeavor. Cash flow statements, balance sheets, and income statements are frequently included in financial projections.

Starting with your revenue predictions, make a sales forecast. Estimate your sales income for every week, month, or quarter, accounting for market trends and seasonality. Next, calculate your direct expenses, like the cost of providing a service or the cost of goods sold. To determine your gross profit, deduct these expenses from your sales revenue.

Think about your running costs, such as rent, utilities, payroll, and marketing costs. To determine your operating profit, deduct these costs from your gross profit. Lastly, to determine your net profit, account for any interest or tax costs.

Make balance sheets, which offer a quick glance at the financial status of your company at a certain moment in time, in addition to income statements. The components of a balance sheet are equity (the owner's investment or retained earnings), obligations (such as loans or accounts payable), and assets (such as cash, inventory, or equipment).

Analyze your financial forecasts on a regular basis and contrast them with your actual financial results. You can use this research to spot trends or deviations and modify your financial goals or business objectives accordingly.

In summary
One of the most important steps in starting a successful business is creating a financial strategy. It enables you to project your financial performance, manage spending, estimate income, and keep an eye on cash flow. You may allocate resources wisely, make well-informed decisions, and confidently handle any financial obstacles by creating a thorough financial plan. As your company grows, don't forget to periodically assess and revise your financial strategy to guarantee its continuous applicability and efficacy.

SECURING FUNDING FOR YOUR VENTURE

4.1 Recognizing Various Financing Choices

One of the most important steps in making your business idea a reality is obtaining money. Realizing your entrepreneurial goal can be difficult if you lack sufficient funding. This section will examine the several funding choices that entrepreneurs can choose from and assist you in weighing the advantages and disadvantages of each.

4.1.1 Financed by Oneself

Using your own funds or assets to finance your firm is referred to as self-funding or bootstrapping. By choosing this route, you may stay in total control of your business and stay away from the hassles and responsibilities associated with outside funding sources. If you have enough money or assets from your personal assets to invest in your firm, self-funding may be a good alternative.

One benefit of self-funding is that it keeps all ownership and decision-making authority intact. You can follow your vision without sacrificing your principles or long-term objectives because you are not answerable to outside lenders or investors. In addition, obtaining funds on your own can sometimes be a simpler and quicker procedure than looking for outside assistance.

Self-funding is not without its difficulties, though.

It demands a large personal financial outlay that can prevent you from making additional investments in other spheres of your life. Because you bear full responsibility for the venture's financial success or failure, it can also be perilous. Before selecting this course of action, it is crucial to thoroughly evaluate your financial status and take into account any potential effects on your personal finances.

4.1.2 Family and Friends

Asking friends and relatives for financial support is another typical way that entrepreneurs raise money. This strategy entails reaching out to people who are close to you, who are prepared to invest in your business, and who share your vision. Since friends and family finance frequently offers more flexible terms and cheaper interest rates than formal lenders or investors, it can be a very alluring choice.

It's important to remain professional and handle the situation like a business deal when asking friends and relatives for money. Make sure to present your business plan, financial estimates, and any associated risks in an understandable manner. To safeguard the interests of both parties, precise expectations must be set, and the investment must be formalized through contracts.

Although financial support from friends and family might be a great way to get started, it's important to think about the possible effects on interpersonal ties. Conflicts or tense dynamics can occasionally result from combining personal and professional connections. Setting reasonable expectations, communicating honestly and openly, and making sure that everyone is aware of the benefits and dangers of the investment are all essential.

4.1.3 Angel Capitalists

High-net-worth individuals or groups of them offer early-stage companies financial support in exchange for equity or ownership holdings. These investors are known as angel investors. These investors, who frequently have extensive business experience themselves, can provide your venture with invaluable contacts, industry knowledge, and expertise.

Angel investors usually fund ventures with strong growth prospects and distinctive value propositions. Compared to traditional lenders, they are more likely to take on risk and might be more receptive to funding novel or disruptive concepts. Angel investors can offer access to their professional networks, mentorship, and assistance in addition to financial help.

Having a strong business strategy, a distinct value offer, and a firm grasp of your target market are essential when looking for angel investment. You will have to present your capacity to carry out your business strategy successfully, articulate your vision clearly, and show that there is room for big returns on investment.

4.1.4 Investment Funding

Venture capital (VC) businesses are investment firms that lend money to early-stage and high-potential entrepreneurs in return for ownership holdings or equity. VC firms, as opposed to angel investors, usually make larger investments and concentrate on companies that have the potential for quick growth and scalability.

For businesses, venture capital funding can be transformative, as it offers not just monetary assistance but also connections to a wide range of industry professionals, mentors, and prospective clients. Venture capital firms frequently play a proactive role in the businesses they invest in, offering direction, strategic counsel, and resources to help spur expansion.

Obtaining venture capital money, however, may be difficult and extremely competitive. Venture capital organizations receive a large number of investment proposals; they carefully consider each one, taking into account team experience, market potential, and scalability. To attract venture capital investment, a company needs to have a strong management team, an attractive business model, and a clear route to profitability.

4.1.5 Participating in Crowdfunding

In recent years, crowdfunding has become a well-liked source of finance for business owners. It entails raising modest sums of money from a large number of people, usually via internet channels. Through crowdfunding, business owners may present their concept to a large audience and get financial backing from people who share their vision.

Various forms of crowdsourcing exist, such as donation-based crowdfunding, equity crowdfunding, and reward-based crowdfunding. In reward-based crowdfunding, funders receive a product or prize in return for their financial contributions. Through equity crowdfunding, people can participate in businesses in return for ownership or stock stakes. Using donation-based crowdfunding, money is raised for philanthropic endeavors or social impact initiatives.

Using crowdfunding to evaluate your business idea, attract early interest from customers, and raise startup funds can be quite successful. It also offers a chance to talk directly with potential clients and get their input. But managing a successful crowdsourcing campaign involves thoughtful preparation, efficient promotion, and an engaging supporter narrative.

4.1.6 Loans from Banks

Conventional bank loans are a popular source of capital for business owners. Based on a company's creditworthiness, financial history, and capacity to repay the loan, banks lend money to them. Bank loans can be used to fund a variety of company expenses, including working capital, inventory, and equipment purchases.

A solid credit history, financial predictions, and a well-written business plan are prerequisites for applying for a bank loan. You might be required to offer assets or personal guarantees as a type of security because banks usually need them to secure loans.

Bank loans can give business owners access to funds with flexible payback terms and low interest rates. But the loan approval procedure can be drawn out and necessitate a lot of paperwork. It is essential to thoroughly go over the terms and conditions of the loan and make sure you have a well-thought-out repayment strategy in place for the money you borrowed.

4.1.7 Government Programs and Grants

As a further source of finance, entrepreneurs might look into grants and government initiatives. Grants are non-repayable financial contributions made to assist certain projects or initiatives by foundations, government agencies, or other groups. On the other hand, government programs provide firms in particular sectors or areas with financial support, tax breaks, or subsidies.

Government grants and programs might be a desirable source of capital because they don't need to be repaid and can give your company a big financial boost. But getting grants may be very difficult and time-consuming, and the application process itself can be complicated. It is crucial to fully investigate the grants and programs that are offered, comprehend the requirements for eligibility, and craft an effective application.

In summary
Understanding the various funding alternatives accessible to entrepreneurs is vital for effectively financing their enterprises. Every funding source has pros and cons, and the decision you make will be based on your unique business demands, budgetary constraints, and aspirations. It is crucial to carefully consider each option and choose the one that fits with your long-term vision and growth strategy, regardless of how you choose to finance your business: through grants and government programs, applying for bank loans, approaching angel investors or venture capitalists, crowdfunding, self-funding, or seeking support from friends and family. Recall that obtaining capital is only one aspect of your entrepreneurial journey; you should also concentrate on developing a strong business foundation, carrying out your plan, and providing value to your clients.

4.2 Crafting an Effective Pitch

An effective pitch is an essential tool for every entrepreneur looking to raise money for their business. This is your chance to enthrall possible lenders and investors and persuade them of the worth and promise of your business concept. This section will examine the essential components of an engaging pitch and offer helpful advice on how to structure and present it.

4.2.1 Creating a Narrative Pitch

A captivating story that draws the audience in and clearly conveys your company's distinctive value proposition is the foundation of each successful pitch. Your pitch narrative should be succinct, understandable, and convincing. When you are creating your pitch, keep the following points in mind:

Problem Statement: Begin by stating the issue or pain point that your company is trying to address in plain English. Emphasize the importance of the issue and how it can affect your target audience.

Solution: Outline how your company plan will address the noted issue. Describe how your offering solves the problems and offers clients a special value proposition.

Market Opportunity: Provide evidence of the size and room for expansion of your intended market. Present information and analysis that demonstrate the market opportunity and the need for your product.

Competitive Advantage: Clearly state what makes your company different from the competition and why it will flourish in the marketplace. Emphasize any entry obstacles, intellectual property, or business alliances that provide you with a competitive advantage over rivals.

Business Model: Give an explanation of your business strategy and your intended income stream. Describe the pricing plan, the methods of distribution, and any prospective sources of income that will help your business remain profitable and sustainable.

Showcase any traction and/or milestones that your company has attained thus far. This could involve partnerships, product development, acquiring new clients, or increasing sales. Showcasing these accomplishments proves your company's potential and shows progress.

Team: Give a brief introduction to your group, emphasizing their relevant background and skill set. Investors are funding both your idea and the individuals who created it. Demonstrate that your staff is capable and dedicated to carrying out the business plan successfully.

4.2.2 Putting Your Pitch in Order

It is crucial to organize your pitch in a clear, succinct, and captivating manner after you have created your pitch narrative. The following is a potential pitch structure:

Introduction: Capture the interest of your audience with a compelling opening statement. Give a brief summary of the issue you are trying to solve, along with an introduction to yourself and your company.

Problem Statement: Clearly state the issue or problem that your company is trying to resolve. To highlight the importance of the issue, present persuasive data or anecdotes.

Solution: Outline how your company plan will address the noted issue. Describe how your offering solves the problems and offers clients a special value proposition.

Market Opportunity: Provide evidence of the size and room for expansion of your intended market. Present information and analysis that demonstrate the market opportunity and the need for your product.

Competitive Advantage: Clearly state what makes your company different from the competition and why it will flourish in the marketplace. Emphasize any entry obstacles, intellectual property, or business alliances that provide you with a competitive advantage over rivals.

Business Model: Give an explanation of your business strategy and your intended income stream. Describe the pricing plan, the methods of distribution, and any prospective sources of income that will help your business remain profitable and sustainable.

Showcase any traction and/or milestones that your company has attained thus far. This could involve partnerships, product development, acquiring new clients, or increasing sales. Showcasing these accomplishments proves your company's potential and shows progress.

Team: Give a brief introduction to your group, emphasizing their relevant background and skill set. Investors are funding both your idea and the individuals who created it. Demonstrate that your staff is capable and dedicated to carrying out the business plan successfully.

Financials: Give a summary of your projected revenue, expenses, and profitability at a high level. Give a convincing explanation of your assumptions, be truthful and reasonable, and show how to achieve financial sustainability.

Ask: Clearly communicate your needs to lenders or investors. Be clear about the amount of funding you need and how it will be utilized to promote the expansion of your company, regardless of whether you are looking for a partnership, loan, or equity investment.

Conclusion: Conclude your pitch with a compelling statement that highlights the worth and possibilities of your company. Make a lasting impact and provide a challenge to the audience.

4.2.3 Making Your Proposal

Making a strong pitch is just half the fight; the other half lies in how well you deliver it. The following advice will assist you in making a strong pitch:

Practice: To make sure you are comfortable and confident giving your pitch, go over it several times. Practice in front of a mirror, record your performance, or ask mentors or trusted advisors for feedback.

Be Interesting: To keep your audience interested, use graphics, interesting anecdotes, and narrative tactics. To keep the audience interested, maintain eye contact, speak clearly, and change up the tone and tempo of your speech.

Keep It Brief: Be mindful of the audience's time limits and provide a succinct pitch. Try to keep your pitch between ten and fifteen minutes long to allow for questions and debate.

Answer queries Confidently: Prepare succinct, assured answers to any queries that may come up.

Show off your industry knowledge and experience while remaining receptive to criticism.

Tailor Your Pitch: Make your pitch unique to the demands and preferences of your target audience. Do some research on the lenders or investors you are pitching to, and modify your proposal as necessary.

Be Enthusiastic: Exhibit sincere zeal and love for your company. Entrepreneurs who are enthusiastic and dedicated to their goals have a higher chance of attracting investors.

Be Receptive to Input: Remain receptive to input and helpful critique. Investors could offer insightful comments or recommendations that will help you improve your pitch or company plan.

Recall that making a strong pitch involves more than just selling your idea; it also entails developing rapport with possible lenders or investors and winning their faith and confidence. Rehearse, polish, and modify your pitch in response to criticism and experience. You may improve your chances of getting the money you need to realize your entrepreneurial aspirations by crafting and delivering your pitch skillfully.

4.3 Reaching Out to Lenders and Investors

It's time to approach lenders and investors to get the money you need for your project once you have a strong business plan and a clear idea of what you need to fund. This chapter will walk you through pitching your company to lenders and investors, securing the best possible terms for funding, and approaching them.

4.3.1 Finding Possible Lenders and Investors

Finding the lenders and investors who are most likely to be interested in your company is essential before you approach them. Begin by conducting due diligence and compiling a list of possible lenders and investors that have experience funding or investing in companies that are comparable to yours. Seek out people or organizations that fit your sector, stage of development, and financing needs.

Speak with banks, venture capitalists, private equity firms, angel investors, and other financial organizations. To make connections with possible lenders and investors, go to industry conferences, pitch contests, and networking events. Make use of crowdfunding websites and internet platforms that assist business owners looking for capital.

4.3.2 Developing an Eye-Grabbing Pitch

It's imperative that you have a polished pitch that explains your company's value proposition to lenders and investors. Your pitch should be clear, engaging, and customized to the particular requirements and preferences of your target audience.

Make an elevator pitch first, which is a succinct yet powerful synopsis of your company that can be given in the time it takes to ride an elevator. The problem your company solves, your special solution, the market opportunity, and the possibility for expansion should all be highlighted in your pitch.

Make a thorough pitch deck that offers a more in-depth look at your company in addition to your elevator pitch. Slides from your pitch deck should address the following important topics:

Problem Statement: Clearly state the issue or pain point that your company is trying to solve.

Solution: Describe how and why your product or service is better than current solutions for the stated problem.

Market Opportunity: Describe the size and room for expansion of your target market, together with pertinent consumer demographics and market trends.

Business Model: Explain how your company makes money, including its pricing policies, means of distribution, and tactics for bringing in new clients.

Competitive Advantage: Emphasize the advantages that set your company apart from the competition and your unique selling offer.

Financial projections: Give a reasonable and thoroughly documented assessment of your expected income, expenses, and profitability.

Team: Give a brief introduction to the important members of your team, highlighting their relevant experience and capacity to carry out the business strategy.

Financing Requirements: Clearly articulate the amount of financing you are looking for as well as the ways in which you plan to use it to push milestones and accelerate growth.

Exit Strategy: Talk about your long-term goals for the company and possible ways to let investors go.

Keep in mind to make your pitch deck clear, succinct, and visually appealing. Incorporate charts, graphs, and other visual aids to bolster your main arguments and add interest to the text.

4.3.3 Establishing Trust and Developing Relationships

It takes more than just presenting your company to potential lenders and investors to develop a rapport and earn their trust. Lenders and investors want to know that you have the ability to carry out your plans and are enthusiastic about your firm.

Spend some time learning about the financial history and inclinations of prospective lenders and investors. Adjust your strategy to suit their ideals and areas of interest. Make your communication unique and show that you've done your research.

A useful strategy for establishing connections

with possible lenders and investors is networking. Participate in business communities, go to industry events, and ask your contacts for introductions. Developing a strong network can boost your chances of getting money and open doors to worthwhile prospects.

4.3.4 Outlining Your Company

Being organized, assured, and succinct is crucial when pitching your company to lenders and investors. Repeat your pitch a few times to be sure you can deliver it confidently and with ease.

Take into account the following advice when showcasing your company:

Begin with a compelling opening statement that draws in readers and makes it apparent what issue you are trying to solve.

Clearly state your solution's unique value proposition and why it outperforms competing products.

Employ captivating narratives, case studies, or endorsements to demonstrate the significance and possibilities of your enterprise.

Be ready to respond to inquiries and handle any possible objections or worries. Prepare thoughtful answers for any queries that lenders and investors might have.

Be open and honest about the dangers and difficulties your company may encounter, and show that you have taken steps to reduce those risks.

Demonstrate your love, zeal, and dedication to your company's success. Lenders and investors want to know that you are a committed and tough individual.

4.3.5 Bargaining for Financing Terms
The next stage is to negotiate the funding terms with possible lenders and investors after you have their interest. During this procedure, the investment or loan amount, equity or interest rates, terms of repayment, and any other covenants or conditions are discussed.

It's critical to go into negotiations knowing exactly how much your company is worth and how much money you need. Prepare an explanation of how the funding will be used to spur growth and produce returns, as well as a defense of your value.

To make sure that the financing agreement's terms and conditions are reasonable and advantageous to your company, think about getting legal counsel. It can be difficult to negotiate funding arrangements, so having a legal expert on your side can help safeguard your interests.

Keep in mind that discussions ought to result in a position where all sides are happy with the arrangement. Find a middle ground that satisfies the objectives and standards of the lender or investor as well as yourself, and be willing to make concessions.

In summary

One of the most important steps in obtaining the capital required to realize your business idea is approaching lenders and investors. You may improve your chances of getting the money you need to support your entrepreneurial endeavors by finding possible lenders and investors, developing a strong pitch, establishing connections, and negotiating funding arrangements. Always be ready, self-assured, and tenacious, and keep an open mind to criticism and chances for development.

4.4 Negotiating Funding Terms

Securing funding is a crucial step in turning your business idea into a reality. However, it's not just about finding investors or lenders who are willing to support your venture financially. Negotiating funding terms is equally important to ensure that you are getting the best deal possible and setting your business up for success. In this section, we will explore the key aspects of negotiating funding terms and provide you with valuable insights to help you navigate this process effectively.

4.4.1 Understanding the Funding Landscape

Before diving into the negotiation process, it's essential to have a clear understanding of the funding landscape. Familiarize yourself with the different types of funding options available to entrepreneurs, such as venture capital, angel investors, crowdfunding, bank loans, and government grants. Each option comes with its own set of advantages and disadvantages, so it's crucial to assess which one aligns best with your business goals and needs.

Research and identify potential investors or lenders who have a track record of supporting businesses in your industry or niche. Understanding their investment criteria, preferences, and past deals can give you valuable insights into what they are looking for and how you can tailor your negotiation strategy accordingly.

4.4.2 Setting Realistic Expectations

When entering into funding negotiations, it's important to set realistic expectations. Understand that investors or lenders will be looking for a return on their investment and will want to mitigate their risks. This means that they may require certain terms and conditions that align with their investment strategy.

Be prepared to compromise and find a middle ground that satisfies both parties. Remember that negotiation is a give-and-take process, and being flexible can help you build a strong relationship with your potential investors or lenders.

4.4.3 Key Funding Terms to Consider

During the negotiation process, there are several key funding terms that you should pay close attention to. These terms will have a significant impact on your business's financial health and your ability to grow and succeed. Here are some important terms to consider:

4.4.3.1 Valuation

Valuation refers to the estimated worth of your business. It determines how much ownership you will have to give up in exchange for the funding. Negotiating a fair valuation is crucial to ensure that you are not diluting your ownership too much or undervaluing your business.

4.4.3.2 Equity Stake

Equity stake refers to the percentage of ownership that investors will have in your business. It's important to strike a balance between the amount of funding you need and the percentage of equity you are willing to give up. Consider the long-term implications of diluting your ownership and ensure that you retain enough control over your business.

4.4.3.3 Funding Amount and Tranches

Negotiate the funding amount that aligns with your business needs and growth plans. Additionally, discuss the possibility of receiving the funding in tranches, which means receiving the funds in stages based on achieving certain milestones. Tranches can help mitigate risks for both parties and ensure that the funding is being used effectively.

4.4.3.4 Interest Rates and Repayment Terms

If you are seeking a loan, negotiate the interest rates and repayment terms that are favorable for your business. Consider the impact of interest rates on your cash flow and profitability. Ensure that the repayment terms are realistic and manageable for your business's financial health.

4.4.3.5 Board Representation and Control

In some cases, investors may require a seat on your board of directors or certain control rights. Carefully consider the implications of giving up control and ensure that the investor's expertise and network align with your business's goals and values.

4.4.4 Building a Win-Win Relationship

Negotiating funding terms is not just about getting the best deal for yourself; it's also about building a win-win relationship with your investors or lenders. Show them that you value their expertise and input by actively seeking their advice and involving them in key decision-making processes.

Maintain open and transparent communication throughout the negotiation process and beyond. Be prepared to provide regular updates on your business's progress and address any concerns or challenges that may arise. Building trust and a strong relationship with your investors or lenders can lead to long-term support and potential future funding opportunities.

4.4.5 Seeking Professional Advice

Negotiating funding terms can be complex, especially if you are not familiar with the legal and financial aspects involved. Consider seeking professional advice from lawyers, accountants, or business consultants who specialize in funding negotiations. They can provide valuable insights, help you navigate the legal and financial complexities, and ensure that your interests are protected.

Remember, negotiating funding terms is a critical step in securing the financial resources you need to bring your business idea to life. Approach the negotiation process with a clear understanding of your business's value and needs, set realistic expectations, and be prepared to compromise.

By building a win-win relationship with your investors or lenders, you can set the foundation for a successful and mutually beneficial partnership.

MASTERING THE ART OF MARKETING AND SALES

5.1 Establishing a Powerful Brand

Developing a powerful brand is crucial to your company's success and survival. In addition to making you stand out from the competition, a great brand inspires loyalty and trust in your target market. This section will cover the essential components of creating a powerful brand and provide you with useful tips for creating and enhancing your brand identity.

5.1.1 Establishing Your Brand's Character

Determining your brand identity is a prerequisite to creating a powerful brand. Your brand identity is the distinctive set of components that sets your company apart from competitors in the market. It includes the personality, values, mission, and visual components of your brand. The following steps will assist you in defining your brand identity:

Determine who your intended audience is. Be aware of the needs, tastes, and values of your target market. This will assist you in creating positioning and messaging for your brand that appeals to them.

Describe the values of your brand: Identify the essential principles that your brand upholds. These principles should represent the core of your company and be consistent with the values of your target market.

Create a captivating narrative that effectively conveys the background, objectives, and mission of your company as you craft your brand story. Your brand narrative ought to arouse feelings and establish a stronger connection with your intended audience.

Establish the personality of your brand. Describe the character attributes that best describe your brand. Is your brand serious and polished, or fun and lively? This will affect the communication style and tone of voice of your brand.

Create a visual brand for yourself. Select visual components such as a logo, color scheme, typography, and other items that capture the essence of your brand. Brand awareness depends on visual branding being consistent across all touchpoints.

5.1.2 Creating Awareness of the Brand

Creating brand awareness is the next stage after defining your brand identity. The degree to which your target audience is aware of and recalls your brand is known as brand awareness. The following tactics can assist you in increasing brand awareness:

Brand uniformity: Make sure that your logo appears consistently on your website, social media accounts, packaging, and promotional materials, among other marketing platforms. Maintaining consistency fosters client trust and facilitates easy brand recognition.

Material marketing: Provide insightful and captivating material that speaks to your target audience and is consistent with your brand values. Blog entries, films, podcasts, and social media content might all fall into this category. Address the concerns of your audience and share your knowledge.

Social media marketing: Make use of social media channels to interact with your target market, tell the story of your company, and start dialogues. To increase your reach and create a community around your company, combine paid and organic marketing techniques.

Influencer collaborations: Work with well-known figures in the field or influencers whose beliefs coincide with your own and who enjoy a sizable fan base. Their support may contribute to a rise in audience credibility and brand visibility.

Public relations: To get press attention for your brand, cultivate connections with bloggers, journalists, and other media sources. Product reviews, guest posts, and interviews can all fall into this category. Good media coverage has the power to dramatically increase brand recognition.

5.1.3 Fostering Brand Adherence
Developing a loyal customer base is essential for long-term success. In addition to making repeat purchases, devoted consumers also function as

brand ambassadors, generating goodwill and drawing in new clients. The following are some methods to encourage brand loyalty:

Exceptionally high-quality customer service should be offered at all points of contact. Inquire with customers as soon as possible, handle problems effectively, and go above and beyond to meet and surpass their expectations.

Customize your communications: Address each consumer specifically with offers and marketing materials that are tailored to their interests and past purchases. Customization gives consumers a feeling of value and exclusivity.

Reward devoted consumers by putting in place a loyalty program that provides discounts, rewards, or special benefits to those who return. This promotes customer loyalty and provides an incentive for customers to select your brand over rivals.

Interact with your audience: Use social media to actively interact with your audience, reply to messages and comments, and promote user-generated material. This creates a stronger bond with your brand and a feeling of community.

Request and act upon customer input: Consistently ask for feedback from your clients in order to enhance your offerings in terms of goods and services as well as the general customer experience. Behaving as though you respect their viewpoints fosters loyalty and trust.

5.1.4 Handling the Image of a Brand

In the current digital era, maintaining and safeguarding the reputation of your brand is crucial. A bad reputation can seriously hinder the expansion and profitability of your company. The following are some methods for successfully managing the reputation of your brand:

Keep an eye on online conversations: To find out what people are saying about your brand, keep an eye on social media, online forums, and reviews of websites. Reactions to unfavorable evaluations or remarks should be handled quickly and expertly.

React to reviews and comments: Whether a customer leaves a negative or favorable review, respond to them. Confirm any concerns or difficulties brought up in unfavorable reviews, and thank clients for their positive feedback. Demonstrate that you are paying attention and acting.

Be open and truthful. Admit any errors or shortfalls in your messages and act with transparency. Establishing credibility and trust with your audience is mostly dependent on your sincerity and genuineness.

Develop good ties with media and influencers: Nurture connections with media outlets, journalists, and influencers. To guarantee favorable coverage and combat any possible bad news, give them useful and reliable information about your brand.

Handle crises proactively: React swiftly and openly in the case of a crisis or bad press. Assume responsibility, express how you plan to address the problem, and show that you are dedicated to making things right.

It takes time, effort, and consistency to develop a successful brand. You can build a strong and enduring brand that connects with your target market and propels the success of your company by defining your brand identity, creating brand awareness, encouraging brand loyalty, and managing your brand reputation.

5.2 Determining the Target Market

Knowing who your target consumer is and what they want is essential to selling and marketing your goods and services. They are the people or organizations who are most likely to be considering what you have to offer and are prepared to pay for it. You may increase the likelihood of attracting and keeping your target client base by identifying them and then customizing your marketing methods and messaging to speak to them.

5.2.1 Creating the Perfect Client Profile

Establishing the perfect client profile is crucial before you can start defining your target audience. The qualities and attributes of the people or groups that are most likely to become your clients are reflected in this profile. First, take into account the following elements:

Demographics: This comprises details on location, age, gender, income bracket, degree of education, and occupation. You may better target your marketing efforts at your target clients by knowing their demographic composition.

The attitudes, interests, values, and lifestyles of your target market are referred to as psychographics. You can craft marketing messages that connect with consumers more deeply if you have a thorough grasp of their motivations, preferences, and behaviors.

Needs and Pain Points: Determine the precise requirements, difficulties, and pain points that your intended clientele is facing. By framing your offering as a remedy to their issues, you can make it seem more appealing and pertinent to them.

Buying Behavior: Take into account the methods your intended audience uses to decide what to buy. Are they more concerned with quality or price? Which do they prefer: in-person or internet shopping? Knowing their purchasing patterns will enable you to choose the best methods and approaches for connecting with and interacting with them.

You can develop a thorough and in-depth ideal customer profile that will direct your marketing and sales activities by integrating these elements.

5.2.2 Researching the Market

It is crucial to carry out market research to confirm and improve your comprehension of your target client base after you have established your ideal customer profile. Obtaining and examining information on your target market's interests, actions, and shopping patterns is known as market research. The following are some techniques for carrying out market research:

Surveys: Design online or offline surveys to acquire input and understanding from your intended clientele. To learn more about their desires, ideas, and preferences, ask them questions that will help you comprehend their actions and intentions.

Interviews: To obtain qualitative data, have one-on-one interviews with your target market. This can offer insightful information about their preferences, purchasing patterns, and problem issues.

Focus Groups: Assemble participants for focus

groups that meet the demographics of your target market. Encourage conversation and get input on your offering, the customer's entire experience, and their level of happiness.

Data analysis: To learn more about the habits and preferences of your target market, examine already-existing data, such as customer purchase histories, website analytics, and social media participation.

You may improve your awareness of your target market, define your ideal client profile, and make well-informed choices regarding your marketing and sales tactics by carrying out in-depth market research.

5.2.3 Developing Personas for Customers
Customer personas are made-up depictions of your ideal clients that assist you in comprehending and connecting with them. They can direct your marketing and sales activities because they are based on the information and perceptions gained from market research. To construct consumer personas, follow these steps:

Analyze Data: Look over the information gathered from market research to find trends and traits that your target market shares. Examine commonalities in needs, pain spots, psychographics, and demography.

Sort Similar Customers: Using their similarities, divide up your target market into smaller groups.

You might have, for instance, a market segment of young professionals who value convenience and are prepared to pay more for it, and another of frugal families who place affordability first.

Give Them Names and Personalities: Give each consumer segment a name and make up a fictional personality. This makes it easier to relate to and humanize your target audience when creating marketing campaigns and messaging.

Establish Objectives and Difficulties: Establish the objectives and difficulties that every consumer category is probably going to face. This will assist you in presenting your product or service as a remedy for their particular problems and wants.

Write Narratives: Craft stories or narratives that highlight the common experiences and trajectories of your target audience. This will assist you in comprehending their attitudes, actions, and methods of making decisions.

You can gain a better understanding of your target market and adjust your marketing and sales strategies to suit their unique requirements by developing customer personas.

5.2.4 Streamlining Your Advertising Approaches

To effectively reach and engage your target customers, it's critical to optimize your marketing strategy after you've established customer profiles and identified your target market. Here are some tactics to think about:

focused advertising: Develop focused advertising campaigns by utilizing the knowledge gathered from your consumer personas. This entails choosing the most appropriate media, messaging, and imagery to successfully reach your target audience.

Material marketing: Provide insightful and useful material that speaks to the needs and problems of your target audience. Blog entries, films, podcasts, and social media content might all fall into this category. You may become an authority in your field and gain the trust of your target audience by producing high-quality content.

Social Media Marketing: Use social media sites to interact with potential clients and increase brand recognition. Determine which social media platforms are most often used by your target audience, then produce content that appeals to them.

Influencer marketing: Assist influencers who enjoy a sizable following from your intended audience. By doing this, you may expand your audience and gain the respect and confidence of your intended market.

Personalization: Adapt your offers and marketing messaging to the unique requirements and tastes of your target market. Utilize the information and understanding obtained from market research to craft experiences that are tailored to their needs.

You may boost the efficacy of your marketing campaigns and draw in and keep devoted clients by honing your marketing techniques in light of your understanding of your target audience.

Recall that the process of finding target clients is continuous. To keep your marketing and sales activities current and successful as your company expands, it's critical to periodically review and refresh your understanding of your target market.

5.3 Formulating Powerful Marketing Plans

Any firm must prioritize marketing since it is essential to drawing in and keeping clients. Effective marketing strategy development is crucial for business owners who want to expand their operations and build a strong brand identity. This part will examine the essential elements of creating effective marketing strategies and how to use them to propel business expansion.

5.3.1 Recognizing Your Ideal Customer

Gaining a thorough understanding of your target market is essential before creating any kind of marketing strategy. This entails figuring out the requirements, tastes, and habits of your target clientele. You may make more informed marketing decisions by collecting information about your target audience and conducting market research.

Begin by drafting fictionalized descriptions of your ideal clientele, or buyer personas. Along with psychographic features like interests, values, and motives, these personas should have demographic data like age, gender, location, and income level. You can effectively adjust your marketing messages and methods to resonate with your target market by studying their qualities.

5.3.2 Clarifying What Makes Your Offer Different
Your unique value proposition (UVP) must be clearly defined if you want to stand out in a crowded market. What makes your company unique and communicates the value you provide to clients is your unique value proposition (UVP). The advantages and benefits that clients can anticipate from selecting your goods or services should be spelled out in detail.

Take into consideration the following inquiries while you create your UVP:

What issue is resolved by your offering?
What distinguishes your product from rivals?
What particular advantages do clients have when they choose your company?
Creating a strong value proposition (UVP) can help you stand out from the competition and draw in clients. It will also act as a basis for your marketing

messaging.

5.3.3 Selecting Appropriate Marketing Channels

It's time to select the best marketing channels to reach your audience efficiently after you have a firm grasp of your target market and have established your unique value proposition. A wide range of marketing channels are at one's disposal, such as public relations, digital platforms, traditional advertising, and direct marketing. The secret is to choose the channels based on the tastes and habits of your target audience.

Because digital marketing is so accessible and affordable, its popularity has grown. It encompasses a range of platforms, including paid internet advertising, email marketing, social media marketing, content marketing, and search engine optimization (SEO). It's crucial to assess which channels work best for your particular company and sector, though.

Depending on your target demographic and industry, traditional marketing mediums like print, radio, television, and outdoor advertising can still be useful. Press releases and media attention are examples of public relations initiatives that can help increase brand awareness and reputation.

5.3.4 Producing engaging content: content

marketing has emerged as a potent instrument for business owners looking to interact with their target market and foster brand loyalty. You may draw in potential clients and position yourself as an industry expert by producing insightful and timely content.

Take into account the following content marketing techniques:

Blogging: Keep a blog on your website where you may post updates, advice, and market insights. This raises the search engine rankings of your website while also benefiting your viewers.

Social media: Create a plan for sharing content, interacting with users, and creating a brand community on social media. You should adapt your material to the specific features and audience of each social media site.

Video marketing: Produce interesting videos to provide client endorsements, highlight your goods or services, or offer instructional material. Video content is becoming more and more common and may be shared on many different platforms.

Email marketing: To keep your audience informed and interested, create an email list and send out newsletters or promotional emails on a regular basis. Make your emails more appealing and relevant by personalizing them.

Recall that offering value to your audience and establishing yourself as a reliable source in your field are essential components of a successful content marketing strategy.

5.3.5 Examining and Quantifying the Outcomes

Analyzing and measuring the outcomes of your efforts is essential to guaranteeing the efficacy of your marketing initiatives. Tracking key performance indicators (KPIs) that support your marketing objectives and goals is part of this.

Several typical marketing KPIs consist of:

Website Traffic: Keep tabs on how many people visit your website and follow their path of travel. This will assist you in determining which marketing avenues are bringing in the most customers.

Conversion Rate: Calculate the proportion of website visitors who complete a desired activity, such as buying something or submitting a form. This will assist you in assessing how well your website and marketing materials are doing.

Customer Acquisition Cost (CAC): Determine the total cost of gaining a new client, taking marketing expenditures into account. This will assist you in figuring out how profitable your marketing campaigns are.

Return on Investment (ROI): Calculate how much money you will make from your marketing expenditures. Examine the difference between the money your marketing efforts bring in and the expenses you incur.

Through consistent analysis and measurement of your marketing outcomes, you may pinpoint opportunities for enhancement and make informed decisions based on facts to maximize your tactics.

In summary
In order to expand their enterprises and create a strong brand identity, entrepreneurs must develop efficient marketing tactics. You can create marketing strategies that propel business growth and success by knowing your target market, developing your unique value proposition, selecting the best marketing channels, producing engaging content, and evaluating the outcomes. Recall that marketing is a continual process; therefore, to maintain your advantage in a fast-paced and cutthroat industry, you must constantly assess and improve your tactics.

5.4 Applying Sales Strategies

Any business owner hoping to expand and boost revenue has to know how to close deals. We will look at a number of different approaches and techniques in this area to help you market your goods and services successfully. Understanding your target market, forming trusting connections, and closing deals are just a few of the reasons why it's critical for your business to grasp sales strategies.

5.4.1 Recognizing Your Ideal Clientele
A thorough understanding of your target market is essential before you can market your goods or services successfully. This entails determining their requirements, inclinations, and areas of discomfort. Obtaining consumer feedback and conducting market research can yield insightful information about the reasons behind consumers' purchasing decisions.

You can adjust your sales strategy to fit the unique needs of your target clients once you have a thorough grasp of them. This could entail crafting a distinctive value proposition that appeals to your target market, tailoring your marketing messaging, and changing up your offers of goods and services.

5.4.2 Establishing Credibility and Trust
Establishing credibility and trust with prospective clients is crucial to achieving success in sales. A company that people believe to be reliable and trustworthy has a higher chance of getting business. There are numerous approaches to building credibility and trust:

Keep your word and make sure you constantly provide superior goods or services that either match or surpass your clients' expectations. This will promote favorable word-of-mouth recommendations and reputation-building.

Offer social proof by showcasing client success stories, case studies, and testimonials to prove the worth and efficacy of your products. This can allay any uncertainties or worries that prospective clients might have.

To establish thought leadership, use content marketing, speaking engagements, or industry magazines to share your knowledge, ideas, and skills. This will help you establish yourself as an authority in your field. With your target audience, this might aid in establishing credibility and trust.

Provide warranties or guarantees: You can allay prospective clients' worries about the efficacy or caliber of your goods or services by offering warranties or guarantees. This demonstrates your willingness to stand behind your offering and your level of trust in it.

5.4.3 Skillful Listening and Communication
Successful selling is mostly dependent on having effective listening and communication abilities. It is crucial to pay attention to the demands and concerns of potential clients while interacting with them. This enables you to customize your sales pitch and answer any concerns or reluctances they might have.

Effective communication not only entails

listening but also precisely stating the advantages and worth of your goods and services. This entails emphasizing how your products or services may address their unique demands, solve their problems, or enhance their lives. Avoid using jargon or technical phrases that could alienate or confuse your target audience in favor of language that speaks to them.

Additionally, it's critical to modify your communication approach for every single client. While some clients might respond better to a more relaxed and personable tone, others might prefer a more formal and professional approach. You can make a stronger connection and generate rapport by being aware of and accommodating of their communication preferences.

5.4.4 Creating Connections and Offering Top-Notch Customer Support

Developing a solid rapport with your clients is essential to long-term success. This entails going above and beyond the first transaction to provide outstanding customer service for the duration of the customer relationship. Here are some tactics to think about:

Customize the encounter: Adapt your communications and interactions to each unique customer. Pay attention to their wants and concerns, remember their preferences, and address them by name.

Be approachable and receptive. Answer consumer questions as soon as possible, whether they come in via social media, email, or phone. Make it simple for clients to get in touch with you by offering a variety of contact options.

Expect the unexpected and surpass it. To surpass your customers' expectations, go above and beyond. This can be extending more assistance, giving out surprise bonuses or discounts, or taking proactive measures to resolve any problems or worries.

Get input and act upon it. Ask for feedback from your clients on a regular basis to learn about their satisfaction levels and pinpoint areas that need work. Take note of their suggestions and adjust as needed to improve the clientele's experience.

Strong bonds and top-notch customer care will help you cultivate devoted clients who will not only keep coming back to buy from you but also act as brand ambassadors.

5.4.5 Sealing the Offer

The last phase in the sales process is closing the transaction. It entails overcoming the customer's reservations and objections in order to convince them to buy. Here are some strategies to assist you in successfully closing the deal:

Respond to objections: Pay attention to the customer's worries and complaints, then directly answer them. To allay their concerns, give more details, make suggestions, or share success stories.

Instill a sense of urgency: By instilling a sense of urgency, you can motivate the customer to act. To do this, you can highlight scarcity, give deals that are only valid for a short period of time, or underline the advantages of acting now.

Offer incentives: Offer incentives to encourage a buyer to buy something. Discounts, freebies, or special offers that enhance the value of their purchase can fall under this category.

Don't be scared to ask for the sale. Make an offer. The customer should be guided through the purchasing process, and the next steps should be communicated clearly.

Recall that closing a sale does not require being forceful or confrontational. It is about being aware of the requirements and worries of the client and giving them the information and assistance they require in order to make an educated choice.

Using successful sales strategies is essential to your company's success. You may improve your sales and propel the expansion of your business by knowing your target market, establishing credibility and trust, developing strong interpersonal skills, cultivating connections, and closing agreements with efficiency.

BUILDING AND LEADING A HIGH-PERFORMING TEAM

6.1 Finding and Selecting the Best Talent

Developing a high-performing staff is essential to your company's expansion and success. You can't do everything as an entrepreneur by yourself, so finding the right people to work with is crucial to making your vision a reality. This section will discuss the hiring and recruitment procedures that will help you find the proper people to help your business succeed.

6.1.1 Clarifying the Needs of Your Team

It's critical to specify the roles and duties that need to be filled within your company before you start the hiring process. Determine the precise credentials and experience needed by first evaluating the knowledge and abilities needed for each role. Think about your company's long-term objectives and how each position will help it reach those objectives.

Additionally, consider your organization's principles and culture. Employing people who are passionate about your sector and who share your company's values will improve the work environment as a whole and help your firm succeed.

6.1.2 Drawing Great Talent

You must develop an employer brand that effectively communicates your company's vision, core principles, and differentiators if you want to draw in top talent. Provide a job description that is easy to read and understand, emphasizing the duties, requirements, and advantages of the role. Make the most of this chance to present the culture of your business and the growth and development possibilities you provide.

Promote your job openings through a variety of venues, including professional networking sites, social media platforms, and online job boards. Make the most of your professional network and urge your staff to recommend possible hires. Additionally, if you want to network with brilliant people who are actively looking for new chances, think about going to industry events and job fairs.

6.1.3 Candidate screening and interviews
After receiving applications for the job, it's time to evaluate and speak with potential individuals. Examine their cover letters and resumes first to gauge their experience and credentials. Seek out candidates with a passion for your company, a proven track record of accomplishment, and relevant industry experience.

After that, have preliminary phone or video interviews to determine each candidate's appropriateness for the position in more detail. Create a list of typical questions to aid in assessing their qualifications, background, and cultural fit. Throughout the interview, focus on their ability to communicate, solve problems, and fit in with your company's ideals.

Choose a few prospects from the first round of interviews to invite for follow-up interviews. These interviews offer a chance to evaluate the candidates' teamwork abilities, interpersonal skills, and general fit with your company. Think of holding panel interviews so that different team members can assess the applicants and offer their opinions.

6.1.4 Evaluating Cultural Fit

A crucial factor to take into account when recruiting new team members is cultural fit. Even if an applicant meets all the requirements and has relevant expertise, they might not succeed in your firm if their values conflict with yours. Examine the candidate's work ethic, values, and capacity for environmental adaptation during the interview process.

To gain insight into the candidate's cultural fit, think about including current team members in the interview process. Inquire about their capacity to collaborate with others and whether they have the same values as your organization. Additionally, think about contacting former coworkers or bosses for references in order to get their opinions.

6.1.5 Onboarding and Retaining Talent Having a well-organized onboarding procedure in place is crucial after you've chosen the best applicant for the job. The new team member will be able to seamlessly integrate into your company and start contributing right away with the support of this approach. Give them the guidance, tools, and assistance they need to succeed in their position.

Establish a culture at work that values development, acknowledgment, and work-life harmony if you want to attract and keep top talent. Provide opportunities for growth and promotion for professionals inside your company. Maintain open lines of communication with your team members to learn about their requirements and resolve any issues they may be experiencing. To inspire them and keep them on board, acknowledge and thank them for their contributions.

In summary
Building a high-performing workforce that can support the expansion and success of your company starts with finding and hiring the appropriate people. You may put together a team that will support you in achieving your entrepreneurial objectives by outlining your needs, luring top talent, screening and interviewing applicants, determining cultural fit, and putting in place efficient onboarding and retention procedures. Recall that your staff is the foundation of your business, so spending time and energy finding the ideal candidates will pay dividends in the end.

6.2 Fostering a Positive Environment at Work

Establishing a healthy work environment is critical to every company's success and expansion. Not only can a positive work culture increase employee engagement and satisfaction, but it also fosters productivity and creativity. This section will examine the essential components of a positive workplace culture and offer doable tactics for fostering it in your company.

6.2.1 The Value of a Positive Work Environment
A flourishing and peaceful workplace is built on a positive work culture. Employee collaboration, trust, and a sense of belonging are encouraged, and this raises job satisfaction and retention rates. Employees are more likely to be driven, effective, and dedicated to the objectives of the company when they feel appreciated and supported.

Moreover, open communication, creativity, and invention are encouraged in a healthy work environment. It promotes risk-taking, idea sharing, and creative thinking among staff members, which fosters ongoing development and progress. Because they feel at ease working together and supporting one another, employees who have a positive work culture are also more cooperative and team players.

6.2.2 Essential Components of a Positive Work Environment

It's critical to concentrate on the following essential components in order to develop a positive work culture:

1. Unambiguous and common values

Establishing a positive work culture requires establishing shared and unambiguous ideals. Within the organization, these values act as guiding principles that influence behavior and decision-making. A positive work environment is facilitated by employees feeling purposeful and directed when they share the organization's ideals.

2. Openness and Credibility

Integrity and trust are the cornerstones of a productive workplace. It is the responsibility of leaders to create a culture that values and supports trust. This can be accomplished through having honest and open lines of communication, involving staff members in decision-making, and giving them regular praise and feedback. Employee engagement and commitment to their work are more likely when they have faith in their leaders and believe that their opinions are valued.

3. Welfare of Employees

A positive work culture must be established by placing a high priority on employee well-being.

This entails encouraging a work-life balance, offering chances for career advancement, and providing assistance with one's physical and emotional well-being. Employees are more likely to be driven, effective, and content in their positions when they feel valued and supported.

4. Cooperation and Coordination
Building a positive work culture requires promoting cooperation and teamwork. Cross-functional teams can be formed, open communication and knowledge sharing encouraged, and cooperative efforts acknowledged and rewarded. The overall work culture is improved when people collaborate to achieve a similar objective because it fosters a sense of camaraderie and shared purpose.

5. Ongoing Education and Development
Building a culture of ongoing learning and development is crucial to establishing a productive workplace. This can be achieved by encouraging staff members to take on new challenges and responsibilities, establishing mentorship programs, and creating opportunities for skill development. When workers are given the chance to develop, they feel appreciated and inspired, which fosters a healthy work environment.

6.2.3 Techniques for Fostering a Positive Work Environment
After discussing the fundamental components of a positive work culture, let's talk about some

doable tactics for fostering one inside your company:

1. Set a good example.
It's critical for a leader to set an example for their team members by modeling the attitudes and conduct they find admirable. In your relationships with your team, exhibit open communication, honesty, and trust. Express gratitude for their efforts and offer helpful criticism. Your staff will be motivated to follow your example if you lead by example.

2. Encourage candid dialogue.
Establish an environment of open communication where staff members are at ease sharing their thoughts, worries, and suggestions. To get feedback from your staff, hold frequent team meetings, one-on-one conversations, and anonymous suggestion boxes. Pay attention to what they have to say, and take care of any problems or difficulties they may be having. You can establish an inclusive and cooperative work atmosphere by encouraging open communication.

3. Acknowledge and honor
Acknowledge and compensate staff members for their efforts and accomplishments. Honor achievements, provide credit for outstanding work, and offer chances for development and promotion. This raises spirits among staff members and fosters a supportive workplace environment where workers are respected and feel

valued.

4. Promote a balanced work-life schedule.
Encourage employees to take breaks and vacations, give flexible work schedules, and provide tools for stress and wellbeing management to help foster a work-life balance. Encourage staff members to put self-care first and establish a welcoming workplace where they can successfully manage their personal and professional lives.

5. Make an investment in staff training.
By offering training courses, workshops, and mentorship opportunities, you can make an investment in your staff members' professional growth. Encourage the development of their careers and assist them in learning new things. By supporting staff development, you not only increase their potential but also show that you care about their achievement and welfare.

6. Encourage a feeling of acceptance.
By encouraging diversity and inclusion throughout your company, you can help people feel like they belong. Encourage staff members to value their distinct viewpoints and experiences. Encourage an inclusive workplace where all employees are treated with dignity and have a sense of support. You can establish a productive workplace culture where staff members may flourish and give their all by encouraging a sense of belonging.

In summary

Establishing a positive work culture is critical to your company's success and expansion. It is possible to create a productive workplace where staff members feel inspired, involved, and empowered by emphasizing fundamental components including transparency, trust, employee well-being, teamwork, and ongoing learning. Put the tactics covered in this section into practice to develop a productive workplace environment that encourages creativity and long-term success.

6.3 Gaining Capabilities for Effective Leadership

Building strong leadership abilities as an entrepreneur is essential to the prosperity and expansion of your company. Your team's performance, motivation, and general productivity will all be directly impacted by your capacity to inspire and lead them. This part will cover the essential ideas and methods for cultivating strong leadership qualities that will help you create and manage a productive team.

6.3.1 Comprehending Different Leadership Styles

There is a wide range of leadership styles, and it is critical to comprehend the various philosophies and how they affect your team. Certain leaders may take on an authoritarian approach, in which they decide without seeking input from their team members. Although this approach might be useful in some circumstances, it can also result in a lack of creativity and involvement from employees.

By including team members in the decision-making process, democratic leadership, on the other hand, promotes a sense of empowerment and ownership. Increased employee happiness and inventiveness may result from this approach. To effectively lead, you must nevertheless find a balance and modify your approach depending on the demands of your group and the circumstances.

6.3.2 Effective Communication

One of the most important aspects of leadership is effective communication. Communicating your vision, objectives, and expectations to your team members in a clear and concise manner is crucial. Maintain open lines of communication with your staff, offering suggestions and resolving any problems that may come up.

Another essential element of good communication is active listening. Give careful consideration to the opinions, worries, and suggestions of your team members. You may show respect and foster an atmosphere where everyone feels heard and appreciated by actively listening.

6.3.3 Setting an Example

Your deeds speak louder than words when you are a leader. Setting an example for your team members to follow entails modeling the attitudes and conduct you demand of them. Show that you have a great work ethic, integrity, and accountability. Demonstrate to your colleagues that you are prepared to get in and work alongside them.

Setting a good example for your team members encourages them to do the same, which fosters a culture of excellence and high output. Your team's attitudes and behavior will be influenced by your actions, which will also set the tone for the entire organization.

6.3.4 Empowering your team Providing your team with the freedom to decide for themselves and accept accountability for their work entails assigning them tasks and granting them autonomy. Their motivation and job satisfaction rise as a result, and they are also able to advance their abilities and skills.

Give your team members the tools, encouragement, and direction they need to be successful in their positions. Motivate them to take chances, grow from their errors, and keep getting better. You can foster a culture of trust, cooperation, and creativity by giving your team more authority.

6.3.5 Establishing Trust and Relationships

Effective leadership requires you to establish trusting bonds with your team members. Spend some time getting to know your teammates personally so you may better comprehend their goals, shortcomings, and talents. Demonstrate sincere concern for their career advancement and well-being.

The cornerstone of any productive team is trust. Maintain integrity in your relationships, communicate openly, and behave consistently. Open communication, teamwork, and a healthy work atmosphere will all be facilitated by trust.

6.3.6 Mentoring and Coaching

It is your duty as a leader to assist your team members in their personal and professional development. Take a coaching and mentoring stance, offering direction, criticism, and chances for growth and learning.

Have regular meetings with your team members to go over their objectives, achievements, and any difficulties they may be having. Give them helpful criticism and assist them in identifying areas where they may improve. By supporting their growth, you not only improve their abilities but also foster devotion and loyalty.

6.3.7 Handling Disagreements

There will always be conflict in any group or organization. It's critical for leaders to resolve disputes amicably and quickly. Establish a free-flowing, safe space where team members can voice their worries and work out disagreements.

When disagreements emerge, pay attention to what each side has to say and work to come up with a win-win solution. Promote direct and honest communication, and step in to settle disputes as needed. By settling disputes amicably, you promote a happy and peaceful workplace.

6.3.8 Ongoing Education and Development

Being a leader is an ongoing process of learning and development. Keep abreast of the most recent developments in the field, best practices, and leadership philosophies. To determine your areas for improvement, get input from mentors, peers, and team members.

Make an investment in your own professional and personal growth by taking advantage of networking events, workshops, and courses. You can lead by example for your team and maintain the applicability and effectiveness of your leadership abilities by always learning and developing.

In summary

Having strong leadership abilities is crucial to assembling and managing a productive team. You will be well-equipped to lead your company to success if you comprehend various leadership philosophies, communicate clearly, set an example for others, empower your team, cultivate relationships and trust, provide coaching and mentorship, handle dispute resolution, and never stop learning and growing. Recall that effective leadership involves inspiring and enabling others to realize their greatest potential as much as managing them.

6.4 Inspirational and Encouraging Your Team:

The success of any entrepreneurial endeavor depends on the development and leadership of a high-performing team. You cannot succeed as an entrepreneur by yourself; thus, it is crucial to assemble a group of gifted people who share your vision and can provide their knowledge and experience to support the growth of your company. But putting together a team is not enough. You must inspire and enable your team members to reach their full potential in order for them to work as a unit. This part will cover tactics and methods for motivating and energizing your staff in order to promote a climate of excellence, innovation, and teamwork.

6.4.1 Establishing a Common Vision

Developing a unified vision is one of the first steps to inspiring and empowering your team. Your team members must comprehend and share your commitment to the mission and objectives of your company. You may motivate your team to work together toward a single objective by outlining your vision and the impact you hope to create in plain terms. Promote candid communication and involve your staff in creating the vision to give them a sense of dedication and ownership.

6.4.2 Clearly Defining Expectations

Setting clear expectations is essential to empowering your staff. Clearly outline each team member's duties, responsibilities, and performance goals. Ambiguity in expectations can cause misunderstanding and annoyance. By being clear, you make it possible for your team members to comprehend their responsibilities and how their contributions fit into the larger objectives of the company. To make sure that everyone is in agreement, communicate and reiterate these expectations on a regular basis.

6.4.3 Granting Independence and Confidence

Allowing your staff the freedom to decide for themselves and accept responsibility for their job is a sign of empowerment. Give your team members the tools and support they need to succeed, and have faith in their ability to make the correct decisions. Micromanagement has the potential to kill creativity and reduce output. Instead, create an atmosphere that encourages people to take chances, learn from their errors, and innovate. You empower your team and foster a culture of growth and accountability when you have faith in them.

6.4.4 Acknowledging and Honoring Success
Rewards and recognition are important tools for inspiring and enabling your staff. Honor both individual and group accomplishments, no matter how modest. Reward and acknowledge your team members' efforts and commitment. There are several ways to be recognized, including through public acclaim, bonuses, promotions, or taking on new duties. Adapt your acknowledgement strategies to the tastes and driving forces of each team member to make them feel important and appreciated.

6.4.5 Fostering Cooperation and Exchange of Ideas
Good teamwork and communication are necessary for a high-achieving group. Encourage team members to communicate in an honest and open manner to create a space where ideas are readily exchanged and discussed. Facilitate possibilities for cooperation by organizing brainstorming sessions, cross-functional projects, and team meetings. Fostering cooperation enables you to use the combined intellect and inventiveness of your group, resulting in creative resolutions and more robust results.

6.4.6 Offering Chances for Development and Growth

Give your staff opportunities for growth and development to empower them. Invest in their career advancement by providing mentorship, conferences, workshops, and training courses. Promote lifelong learning and assist your team members in picking up new abilities and information. By supporting their development, you not only increase their potential but also show that you are dedicated to their long-term success and welfare.

6.4.7 Developing an Upbeat Workplace

Creating a happy work atmosphere is essential to inspiring and enabling your staff. Encourage an inclusive, trustworthy, and respectful culture. Prioritize employee well-being and promote work-life balance. Provide opportunities for social contact and team-building exercises, in addition to a physical workspace that is stimulating and cozy. You can increase team morale, productivity, and overall job satisfaction by fostering a positive work environment.

6.4.8 Setting an Example

When it comes to being a leader and entrepreneur, deeds speak louder than words. Set a good example for your team members by acting in the ways and values you demand of them. Exhibit honesty, a growth mentality, and a strong work ethic.

Be empathetic and attentive to the thoughts and worries of your teammates. Serving as an example for your team encourages them to aspire to greatness and model their behavior after you.

6.4.9 Offering Consistent Support and Feedback

Your team members' development and progress depend on you providing them with regular feedback. Give them constructive criticism in addition to positive criticism to help them become better performers. Provide direction, encouragement, and mentorship to assist them in overcoming obstacles and realizing their full potential. Communicate with your team members on a regular basis to learn about their requirements, resolve any issues, and offer the assistance and resources they require.

6.4.10 Honoring Inclusion and Diversity

Inclusion and diversity foster success and innovation, in addition to being moral requirements. Recognize and celebrate the diversity of viewpoints and experiences that each member of your team brings to the table. Encourage an inclusive atmosphere where everyone is encouraged to share their thoughts and opinions and feels appreciated and respected. A team that embraces diversity and inclusion is more resilient and powerful.

Encouraging and empowering your staff is a continual process that requires constant attention and work. You can develop a high-performing team that is inspired, involved, and empowered to accomplish extraordinary results by establishing a shared vision, laying out clear expectations, granting autonomy and trust, acknowledging accomplishments, promoting collaboration and communication, providing opportunities for growth, fostering a positive work environment, setting an example, offering regular feedback and support, and celebrating diversity and inclusion. Recall that your staff is the foundation of your business, and by supporting their success, you are supporting the success of your enterprise.

LEVERAGING TECHNOLOGY FOR OPERATIONAL EXCELLENCE

7.1 Determining the Need for Technology

In the current digital era, technology is essential to any company's success. It has the capacity to improve productivity, simplify processes, and offer insightful information for making decisions. It is crucial for entrepreneurs to determine their venture's technological requirements and to use the appropriate tools and processes to promote operational excellence. This section will go over the important factors to take into account when determining your company's technology requirements and how to put effective systems and procedures in place to help it run.

7.1.1 Evaluating the Infrastructure of Current Technology

It's critical to evaluate your current technology infrastructure before determining your technological demands. Make an inventory of the systems, software, and hardware that you now have. Assess their efficacy, efficiency, and alignment with your company's objectives. Think about aspects like usability, security, and scalability. This evaluation will give you a general idea of your technological prowess and point out areas in which you can excel.

7.1.2 Outlining Processes and Business Goals

It is essential to match your organization's technological requirements with its overall goals and procedures in order to determine what your needs are. Establish your company's objectives and the main procedures that propel your business's activities first. This could apply to departments like customer support, inventory management, finance, marketing, and sales. Understanding your business's goals and procedures can help you determine the precise technological needs that will support and improve these areas.

7.1.3 Performing a Gap Analysis in Technology

Finding the gaps between your current technological capabilities and the technology needed to meet your business objectives is the goal of a technology gap study. This research assists you in identifying the technological gaps in your company and the necessary solutions. Take into account elements like security, scalability, integration, and functionality. You may create a roadmap for implementation and prioritize your technological needs by carrying out a comprehensive gap analysis.

7.1.4 Looking into Technological Solutions

After determining your technology requirements, it's time to investigate and learn more about the many technological options on the market. Take into account elements like price, ease of use, scalability, functionality, and customer support. Seek out technological solutions that complement your company's goals and workflow. These could include communication platforms, inventory management systems, project management tools, accounting software, and customer relationship management (CRM) software. Spend some time weighing your alternatives to determine which ones best suit your needs.

7.1.5 Tailoring and Combining Technological Solutions

Although off-the-shelf technology solutions can be an excellent place to start, it's crucial to integrate and modify them to meet your unique business needs. To ensure that the solutions meet your needs, collaborate closely with technology consultants or vendors. To guarantee smooth data flow, this may entail integrating several systems, introducing particular features, or modifying workflows. You may maximize the impact of technological solutions on your business operations and their performance by integrating and personalizing them.

7.1.6 Guidance and Assistance

Your workforce has to be properly trained and supported while implementing new technology solutions. Make certain that the training your staff needs to utilize the new technological tools and processes is provided. This can entail holding training sessions, supplying user guides, or making internet information available. Create a support system as well in order to handle any inquiries or technical difficulties that may come up. This can entail hiring specialized IT staff or contracting with a reputable service provider to handle technical support. You can guarantee a seamless transition and optimize the returns on your IT investments by allocating funds for training and assistance.

7.1.7 Observation and Assessment

It's crucial to keep an eye on and assess the technology solutions' performance once you've put them into practice. Determine how well the technology is achieving your goals and producing the expected results on a regular basis. Keep an eye on the key performance indicators (KPIs) that pertain to cost-effectiveness, productivity, efficiency, and customer satisfaction. This will assist you in determining any places that still need work or modification. You can maximize the impact of your IT solutions on your business and make well-informed decisions by tracking and assessing them.

7.1.8 Keeping abreast of technological developments

Since technology is always changing, it's critical for entrepreneurs to keep up with the most recent developments. Keep an eye out for new trends and technology that can be useful to your company. Automation, cloud computing, data analytics, machine learning, and artificial intelligence may all fall into this category. Determine on a regular basis whether the technology solutions you now have in place are still satisfying your needs or if there are any new developments that could provide you with a competitive edge. You can make sure that your IT infrastructure is current and efficient by being knowledgeable and flexible.

In summary, determining your company's IT requirements is a crucial first step toward achieving operational excellence. You can use technology to streamline operations and drive your company toward success by evaluating your current technology infrastructure, matching technology to your goals, conducting a technology gap analysis, investigating and developing custom technology solutions, offering assistance and training, keeping an eye on performance, and keeping abreast of technological developments. In order to unleash the full potential of technology and build your own entrepreneurial empire, embrace it as a strategic facilitator.

7.2 Putting in Place Effective Procedures and Systems

In any firm, efficiency is the key to success. You may optimize production, cut expenses, and streamline your operations by putting in place effective systems and processes. This section will discuss the value of effective systems and procedures and offer doable tactics for putting them into practice.

7.2.1 Evaluating Your Present Procedures and Systems

Evaluate your current operations before putting in place effective systems and procedures. Examine how things are done carefully, note any inefficiencies or bottlenecks, and assess the overall performance of your systems. This evaluation will help you pinpoint areas that need work and act as a starting point for progress.

7.2.2 Simplifying the Process

Streamlining workflow is one of the main objectives of putting effective systems and procedures in place. You may cut out pointless processes and shorten the time it takes to finish a task by streamlining the flow of tasks and information. Start by outlining your present workflow and marking any instances of task duplication or delays. Seek chances to streamline or automate procedures, and think about putting project management tools or software in place to improve coordination and communication.

7.2.3 Procedure Standardization

In order to guarantee consistency and quality in your operations, standardizing procedures is essential. It is possible to reduce errors and boost productivity by putting in place explicit policies and procedures. Create a thorough manual or guide that details your operations and provides step-by-step instructions for every task. This will help with new hire onboarding and training, in addition to acting as a resource for your team.

7.2.4 Putting Technology to Use

When it comes to streamlining procedures and systems, technology is essential. Determine which jobs may be automated with the use of technology in order to increase productivity, accuracy, and efficiency. Think about making an investment in tools or software that can help you manage projects, inventories, customer relationships, and other crucial aspects of your company more effectively. Furthermore, investigate the potential for system integration in order to avoid human data entry and establish a smooth process.

7.2.5 Educating and Motivating Your Group

Effective systems and procedures are only useful if your staff members comprehend and support them. Give your staff thorough training on the new procedures and systems you adopt. Make sure they possess the abilities and know-how needed to use the tools and technology efficiently. Involve your staff in decision-making and welcome their opinions and suggestions for enhancement to empower them. You can develop a motivated, engaged, and efficiency-focused workforce by promoting a culture of continual learning and growth.

7.2.6 Observation and Ongoing Enhancement

It takes constant work to put effective systems and procedures in place. Keep a close eye on how well your systems and procedures are working to spot any areas that could need modification or correction. Gather information and evaluate important indicators to gauge how well your new systems are working. Utilize this knowledge to guide your judgments and carry out any required adjustments. To identify possible areas for improvement, solicit input from your staff and clients. You can make sure that your systems and procedures continue to be successful and efficient by always aiming for perfection.

7.2.7 Cooperation and Interaction

Within your organization, good collaboration and communication are essential to having efficient systems and processes. Encourage cooperation and an atmosphere of open communication throughout various teams and departments. Use platforms and products that promote teamwork and communication, like video conferencing tools, instant messaging applications, and project management software. Within your company, you can increase productivity and efficiency by encouraging openness and information exchange.

7.2.8 Automation and Outsourcing

Automation and outsourcing are two effective methods for increasing productivity. Determine which procedures or duties can be delegated to outside contractors or providers. This might free up time for your staff to concentrate on important business tasks. Furthermore, investigate automation potential by utilizing robotics, AI, and machine learning. Repetitive tasks can be made more efficient, less error-prone, and more efficient overall via automation.

7.2.9 Ongoing Education and Adjustment

Continuous learning and adaptation are essential mindsets for effective systems and processes.

Keep abreast of the most recent developments in technology and business trends to enhance the efficiency of your operations. To learn about best practices and acquire insights from industry professionals, attend conferences, workshops, and seminars. Urge your staff to adopt a culture of innovation and development wherein they are motivated to propose fresh concepts and methods for augmenting productivity.

7.2.10 Case Study: XYZ Company Implements Effective Systems and Procedures

Let's look at the example of XYZ Company to show how effective systems and procedures are implemented in practice. The expanding e-commerce company XYZ Company was having trouble managing its inventory and order fulfillment because of manual procedures and a lack of system integration. An enterprise resource planning (ERP) system that linked XYZ Company's order processing, shipping, and inventory management was put in place to address these problems. They were able to streamline their entire operation, automate order fulfillment, and keep real-time inventory tracking as a result. As a result, the order processing time for XYZ Company was significantly reduced, inventory accuracy was enhanced, and customer satisfaction rose.

In conclusion, streamlining your company's operations requires putting in place effective methods and procedures. You may increase efficiency and production by evaluating your present systems, optimizing workflow, standardizing processes, utilizing technology, and giving your team more authority. Maintaining and increasing efficiency over time requires constant observation, cooperation, and adaptation. Accept the power of effective systems and procedures to help your company reach its maximum potential and succeed.

7.3 Task and Workflow Automation

Automation is a potent tool that may boost productivity, simplify corporate processes, and free up important time and resources. Tasks and workflows can be automated to remove laborious and repetitive procedures, lower mistake rates, and boost output. This section will discuss the advantages of automation and offer doable tactics for integrating it into your company.

7.3.1 Automation's Advantages

There are several advantages to automation for business owners who want to maximize their operations. Here are a few main benefits:

Enhanced Productivity and Efficiency

You may drastically cut down on the time and effort needed to finish activities and workflows by automating them. This frees you and your group to concentrate on more crucial and tactical tasks that promote development and creativity. You may complete more work in less time when repetitive administrative chores, manual data input, and other time-consuming operations are eliminated via automation.

Enhanced Precision and Uniformity

Human error can occur frequently in manual procedures, which can result in expensive errors and inefficiencies. Because automation guarantees precise and consistent task execution, it reduces the possibility of errors. You can lessen the possibility of data entry errors, duplicate entries, and other typical blunders by doing away with manual data input and other manual procedures.

Savings on Costs

By eliminating the need for manual work and lowering the possibility of expensive mistakes, automation can help you save money. You can do away with the need for extra workers or allow current employees to concentrate on more important work by automating monotonous chores. Additionally, by offering insights into your business operations and pointing out areas for development, automation can assist you in finding cost-saving options.

Improved client relationship

Additionally, automation can enhance the customer experience by facilitating smoother operations, more rapid reaction times, and individualized interactions. Automated email marketing campaigns, for instance, might send clients personalized messages according to their interests and usage patterns. Automated customer support solutions have the capability to deliver prompt and precise assistance by responding instantly to frequently asked questions.

7.3.2 Putting Automation to Use in Your Company
Your company needs to prepare and think carefully before implementing automation. Here are some actions to get you going:

Determine which workflows and tasks to automate.
Start by determining which processes and tasks can be automated. Seek out procedures that can be automated to reduce repetition, time spent, and error-proneness. Data entry, report writing, inventory control, and customer service are typical instances.

Assess software and tools for automation.
After determining which processes and tasks need to be automated, look into and assess software and solutions for automation that can assist you in reaching your objectives. Take into account aspects like cost, scalability, compatibility with your current systems, and ease of use. Seek out solutions that provide the capabilities and functionality required to automate the particular procedures you perform.

Create an automation plan.
Create a concise automation strategy that includes your objectives, schedule, and plan of action.

Establish critical milestones to monitor progress and decide which tasks and workflows will be automated first. To guarantee buy-in and support, think about including important stakeholders and staff members in the planning process.

Try and improve.
Make sure the automated workflows and processes are operating as planned by testing them before completing the automation implementation. Determine any problems or opportunities for development and implement the required changes. Maintain constant observation and improvement of your automated processes to maximize efficiency and handle new issues as they arise.

Educate and provide assistance to your group.
To make sure your team knows how to utilize the automated tools and software efficiently, give them training and support. Provide resources and continual training to assist them in adjusting to the changes and maximizing the advantages of automation. Promote cooperation and feedback in order to cultivate a culture of ongoing improvement.

7.3.3 Getting Past Obstacles and Dangers
Even though automation has many advantages, there are still risks and difficulties to be mindful of. The following are some typical obstacles and methods for overcoming them:

Opposition to Change

Because they are worried about losing their jobs or are unsure about their capacity to learn new technology, some workers may oppose automation. Explain the advantages of automation to staff members and include them in the process of designing and executing the plan in order to overcome any opposition. Give them the guidance and assistance they need to acquire the abilities required to operate automated systems.

Issues with Integration and Compatibility

Software and tool integration for automation can be difficult and complex when integrating with current systems. Make sure the automation solutions you select can easily integrate with your present processes and are compatible with your current infrastructure. Speak with IT specialists or, if necessary, look for outside assistance.

Privacy and data security

Sensitive data is used and stored during automation, which raises security and privacy concerns. Put strong security measures in place to safeguard your data, including frequent backups, access controls, and encryption. Respect applicable data privacy laws and make sure your automation tools and software follow best practices in the sector.

Observation and upkeep

For automated systems to continue operating efficiently, constant observation and upkeep are necessary. Review and assess your automated workflows' performance on a regular basis, and adapt as necessary. To take advantage of new features and improvements, keep your automation tools and software updated and upgraded.

In summary
Automation is a potent instrument that may transform your company's operations and spur expansion. Tasks and workflows can be automated to boost productivity and accuracy, cut expenses, and improve customer satisfaction. But effective automation involves thorough planning, assessment of hardware and software, and continual observation and improvement. Leverage automation's potential to unleash the full power of your entrepreneurial empire and embrace it as a strategic advantage.

7.4 Making Decisions Using Data Analytics

Data is king in the modern digital era.

To make wise judgments and grow their firms, entrepreneurs now need to be proficient in the collection, analysis, and interpretation of data. You may better understand client behavior, streamline operations, and spot business possibilities with the use of data analytics. This part will discuss the value of data analytics in decision-making and how to use it to your advantage to obtain a competitive advantage in the marketplace.

7.4.1 Appreciating Data Analytics' Power
Analyzing massive data sets to find trends, correlations, and patterns is known as data analytics. In order to derive valuable insights, it entails gathering data from multiple sources, organizing and cleansing it, and then using statistical tools. Entrepreneurs can make data-driven decisions that are supported by facts rather than conjecture or gut feelings by utilizing data analytics.

Data analytics can offer insightful information in a number of crucial business domains, including:

Analysis of Consumer Behavior
Any firm must have a thorough understanding of its clients. Analyzing client behavior trends, preferences, and purchase habits is possible using data analytics. You may learn more about the requirements and preferences of your clients by looking at data from a variety of touchpoints, including website visits, social media

engagements, and sales transactions. With this information, you can better customize your goods and services to match their needs, raise client satisfaction levels, and increase revenue.

The optimization of operations
You can also optimize your business operations with the use of data analytics. You can find bottlenecks, inefficiencies, and opportunities for improvement by examining data on key performance indicators (KPIs), such as supply chain performance, inventory levels, and manufacturing efficiency. This knowledge can help you cut expenses, improve overall operational efficiency, and streamline procedures.

Analysis of the Market and Competition
Analytics of data can offer insightful information about competition dynamics and market trends. You can analyze market data, including industry studies, consumer surveys, and competition analyses, to find new business possibilities, gauge market demand, and spot developing trends. You can use this information to make well-informed judgments regarding market positioning, pricing schemes, and product development.

7.4.2 Gathering and Examining Information
You must gather and examine pertinent data in order to use data analytics for decision-making in an efficient manner. Here are some actions to get you going:

Find important metrics and information sources. Determine which key KPIs are most important to the success of your company first. These measurements will change based on your business style and industry. For instance, measures like average order value, conversion rate, and website traffic may be significant if you own an online store. Once the important metrics have been determined, find the data sources that will provide you with the information you need. This could be sales data, customer relationship management (CRM) information, or website analytics.

Clear and prepare the information.
An integral part of the data analytics process is data cleaning. It includes fixing typos, standardizing the data format, and eliminating any redundant or unnecessary data. By doing this, the data is guaranteed to be reliable and consistent, enabling insightful analysis. Although it can take some time, data cleaning is essential to getting trustworthy insights.

Utilize statistical methods.
After the data has been cleaned and prepared, statistical methods can be used to analyze it. This could entail the use of data visualization tools to convey the results succinctly and clearly, inferential statistics to make predictions or draw conclusions, or descriptive statistics to summarize the data. You may do these studies with the use of a variety of software and tools, like Google

Analytics, Microsoft Excel, and more sophisticated data analytics platforms.

7.4.3 Making Decisions Based on Data

Only when data analytics produces useful insights and well-informed decisions can it be considered valuable. The following advice will assist you in making data-driven decisions:

Establish specific goals.
Prior to beginning data analysis, be sure your goals are clear. Which particular query are you hoping to have answered? Which issues are you attempting to resolve? You can concentrate your study on the most pertinent facts and derive insights that support your business objectives by establishing specific objectives.

Examine the information in light of the situation. Data analysis involves more than simply math computations; interpretation is also necessary. Take into account the larger context of the data collection when interpreting the data. Are there any outside variables that might have affected the outcomes? Does the data contain any biases or limitations? You can make sure your interpretations are accurate and meaningful by taking the context into account.

Integrate knowledge and experience.
Even though data analytics might offer insightful information, it's crucial to integrate data with your own experience and business knowledge.

While data can be a useful tool in decision-making, it shouldn't take the place of your own discretion and experience. You may make more comprehensive and well-informed decisions by fusing data with your knowledge and experience.

Keep an eye on and refine
Data analytics is a continuous endeavor. Continue to track and evaluate the data to get fresh insights as your company grows and new data becomes accessible. Make use of these insights to improve and hone your plans and techniques. You can maintain an advantage over competitors and adjust to shifting market conditions by consistently utilizing data analytics.

In summary
Data analytics is a potent instrument that can assist business owners in decision-making, operational optimization, and opportunity identification. Entrepreneurs can obtain important insights into consumer behavior, operational effectiveness, and market dynamics by gathering and evaluating pertinent data. Afterwards, strategic decision-making can be influenced by these insights, leading to successful corporate outcomes. Accept the power of data analytics and let it reach new heights in your entrepreneurial endeavors.

SCALING YOUR BUSINESS FOR EXPONENTIAL GROWTH

8.1 Gaining Knowledge of the Growth Mindset

Develop a growth mentality if you want to fully realize the possibilities of your entrepreneurial adventure and grow your company to new heights. A strong belief system known as the growth mindset enables business owners to rise to obstacles, persevere in the face of failure, and always learn and grow. This section will discuss the growth mentality and how it might help your company experience exponential growth.

8.1.1 Adopting a Possibility Mentality

The growth mentality is based on the idea that intelligence and skills can be acquired with commitment and hard work. Growth-minded entrepreneurs regard setbacks as opportunities for improvement and mistakes as priceless teaching moments. They are aware that setbacks are only transient impediments that can be surmounted with tenacity and an openness to change, rather than immovable barriers.

Entrepreneurs that have an attitude of potential make themselves more receptive to fresh concepts, creative fixes, and untapped prospects. They are not constrained by limitations placed on themselves or by the fear of failing. Rather, they face every circumstance with resiliency, curiosity, and a will to grow.

8.1.2 Accepting Adaptation and Ongoing

Development
Long-term success in a corporate environment that is changing quickly requires the capacity to adjust to change. Growth-minded businesspeople accept change as an opportunity for expansion and innovation because they recognize it as an inherent part of the process. They don't hesitate to question the status quo and are always looking for methods to make their procedures, goods, and services better.

Growth mentality is based on the idea of continuous improvement. This kind of thinking is shared by entrepreneurs who are dedicated to improving the value they offer to clients, streamlining operations, and honing their company strategy. They actively look for input, evaluate information, and make adjustments in response to lessons learned from past experiences.

8.1.3 Adopting an Innovative Culture
The foundation of any successful company is innovation. Growth-minded business owners are aware of how critical it is to cultivate an innovative culture within their companies. They push the boundaries of conventional thought, take calculated risks, and foster creative thinking in their teams. They know that innovation can be applied to procedures, marketing plans, and business models in addition to product development.

Entrepreneurs that embrace an innovative culture foster a collaborative atmosphere wherein experimentation is encouraged, new ideas are accepted, and failure is viewed as a necessary step on the path to success. They know that in order to be innovative, one must be prepared to take chances, learn from mistakes, and refine concepts until they produce ground-breaking outcomes.

8.1.4 Accepting Cooperation and Gaining Knowledge from Others

Growth-minded businesspeople understand that they cannot succeed on their own. They actively look for chances to work together and surround themselves with people who have a variety of viewpoints and areas of expertise. They are aware that picking up knowledge from others can help them become more knowledgeable, obtain fresh perspectives, and advance more quickly.

By working together, entrepreneurs can benefit from the combined experience of their peers in the sector, mentors, advisors, and team members. They can take use of other people's talents, close knowledge gaps, and get access to networks and resources that can advance their company. Entrepreneurs foster a culture of ongoing learning and development in their companies by valuing teamwork.

8.1.5 Accepting Stubbornness and Resilience

Establishing a profitable company is not an easy task. It is full of obstacles, setbacks, and ups and downs. Growth-minded businesspeople are aware that resilience and tenacity are necessary traits for conquering challenges and attaining sustained success.

They see setbacks as transitory obstacles that can be surmounted with perseverance and an optimistic outlook, and they see failures as chances to learn and develop. They don't allow failures to define them or stop them from going after their objectives. Rather, they learn from their failures and modify their tactics as they go, using losses as motivation to move on.

8.1.6 Adopting a Long-Term Viewpoint

Growth-minded business owners are aware that creating a successful company requires patience and time. They are motivated by more than just instant satisfaction or quick profits. Rather, they concentrate on the long-term picture and are prepared to make the required time, effort, and financial commitments to reach their objectives.

They are aware that success does not come easily and that perseverance, never-ending learning, and a readiness to adjust to new situations are necessary for it. Temporary setbacks or delayed development do not deter them. Rather, they are prepared to make the required compromises in order to realize their goals and they are steadfast in their commitment to it.

In conclusion, entrepreneurs who want to expand their companies for exponential growth must comprehend and adopt the growth mindset. Entrepreneurs may reach their full potential and succeed in the long run by developing a mindset of possibilities, accepting change and constant improvement, creating an innovative culture, working with others, and exhibiting resilience and tenacity. Accept the growth mentality to fully realize the potential of your entrepreneurial endeavors.

8.2: Creating a Business Model That Is Scalable

For your firm to experience exponential development and reach new heights, you must have a scalable business plan. It enables you to grow your clientele and income without correspondingly raising expenses or resources. This section will cover the essential components of creating a scalable business model and provide you with useful advice for starting your own venture.

8.2.1 Comprehending Scalability

It's important to comprehend what scalability means in the context of entrepreneurship before getting into the details of creating a scalable business model. Scalability is the capacity of an organization to accommodate expansion and rising demand without sacrificing productivity or profitability. With a scalable business strategy, you can grow your company and target more customers without having to shell out a lot of extra money.

8.2.2 Determining Opportunities That Are Scalable

You must find opportunities with the potential for quick growth and scalability in order to create a scalable business strategy. Search for sizable, expanding markets where there is a need for your good or service. Think about how easy it would be to expand your firm to other markets or regions. Consider whether your company can use automation or technology to improve efficiency and streamline processes.

8.2.3 Making Use of Automation and Technology

Technology is essential to creating a company

model that is scalable. You may enhance production, cut expenses, and streamline your operations by utilizing technology and automation. Determine which aspects of your company, such as data analysis, inventory control, and customer service, stand to gain from automation. By putting in place effective systems and procedures, you'll be able to manage growing demand without needing to allocate more resources.

8.2.4 Establishing robust infrastructure

Building a robust infrastructure that can sustain growth and expansion is necessary for a scalable business plan. Invest in dependable technological systems that can manage growing traffic and data storage, like cloud-based platforms. Create a supply chain that is scalable to handle increased production levels and guarantee on-time delivery to clients. Furthermore, concentrate on creating an organizational structure that is scalable so that it can accommodate expansion and handle growing duties with ease.

8.2.5 Establishing Repetitive Procedures

The key to achieving scalability is to design repeatable procedures that are simple to duplicate as your company expands. To maintain efficiency and uniformity, make sure your standard operating procedures and workflows are documented. Automate tedious work and put quality control procedures in place to keep your company operating at the same high standard even as it grows. You may increase your business without compromising the quality of your goods or services by developing repeatable procedures.

8.2.6 Welcome to Innovation and Ongoing Enhancement

Scalability is largely influenced by innovation. Always look for methods to make your processes, goods, and services better in order to keep up with the competition and satisfy changing client demands. Encourage your staff to come up with and execute new ideas by fostering an innovative culture within the company. Accept input from stakeholders and consumers to find areas that need work and modify your business plan accordingly.

8.2.7 Forming Strategic Alliances

Forming strategic alliances can be very helpful in growing your company. Find possible partners who can expand your reach into new markets or distribution channels or who might enhance your current offers. Work together with well-known companies or leaders in the field to take advantage of their resources and knowledge. Build relationships that will benefit both parties, help you expand your audience, and advance your career.

8.2.8 Tracking Important Metrics

It is essential to keep an eye on important indicators that reflect the state and effectiveness of your operations if you want to grow your firm. Decide which metrics—such as revenue growth rate, client lifetime value, or cost of acquisition —are most important to your company. Examine these indicators on a regular basis to see trends, make data-driven choices, and modify your plans as necessary.

8.2.9 Handling Difficulties and Risks

There are dangers and difficulties unique to business scaling. To achieve a smooth growth trajectory, it is critical to foresee and proactively address these difficulties. Evaluate potential risks, including heightened competition, inefficiencies in operations, or budgetary limitations, and create backup plans to help reduce them. To stay ahead of the curve, keep an eye on market trends and adjust your plans as necessary.

8.2.10 Case Studies: Scalable Business Models That Work

This section contains case studies of profitable businesses that have seen exponential growth to give you practical examples of scalable business models. The ideas and approaches these businesses used to grow and achieve extraordinary success will be highlighted in these case studies. You can learn a lot from these examples and use them to inform your own entrepreneurial endeavors.

In summary, creating a scalable business plan is essential to attaining exponential development and expanding your company. You can set up your company for quick growth by comprehending scalability, seeing scalable prospects, using technology, developing repeatable procedures, and welcoming innovation. A scalable business model also requires the development of strategic alliances, the tracking of important indicators, and the skillful management of risks and obstacles. You can create an empire that endures the test of time and pave the path for your own business success by putting these tactics into practice and studying successful case studies.

8.3 Developing New Markets

One of the most important steps in growing your company and attaining exponential development is entering new markets. You can expand your consumer base, diversify your revenue sources, and reach undiscovered customer niches by breaking into new areas. However, there are dangers and hurdles unique to entering new markets. In this part, we will look at the tactics and factors to take into account while successfully growing your company into new markets.

8.3.1 Analysis and Research on the Market

Doing in-depth market research and analysis is crucial before entering new markets. This will assist you in determining prospective business prospects, comprehending the competitive environment, and evaluating the level of demand in the new market for your goods or services. Take into consideration these crucial steps:

Determine your target markets: Choose the markets that have the potential to expand and fit in with your company's objectives. Take into account variables including regulations, cultural differences, economic situations, and demographics.

Examine consumer demand: Determine whether there is a need in the new market for your goods or services. To learn more about potential customers, hold focus groups, interviews, and surveys. To find gaps and opportunities, analyze consumer preferences, rival offerings, and market trends.

Analyze the opposition. Recognize the market's competitive environment. Determine the market shares, pricing policies, methods of distribution, and marketing strategies of your direct and indirect competitors. Make your product stand out from the competition by emphasizing its distinct value propositions and advantages.

Examine the obstacles to entering the new market, including linguistic barriers, cultural differences, legal and regulatory requirements, and distribution difficulties. Create plans to go beyond these obstacles, then modify your business plan to fit the situation.

8.3.2 Strategies for Entering the Market

It's time to create a market entry plan when you've finished your market analysis and research. This plan will specify how you want to join the new market and build your brand there. These are a few typical approaches to entering a market:

Exporting: To begin, export your goods or services to the prospective market. With this tactic, you can raise brand recognition and assess consumer demand without having to make a sizable initial investment. In the new market, you can either export directly or collaborate with distributors or agencies.

Licensing and franchising: Grant local partners in the new market a license to use your intellectual property or a franchise of your business plan. By using this tactic, you may increase your brand's visibility while utilizing your partners' local knowledge and resources.

Joint Ventures and Strategic Partnerships: Establish joint ventures or strategic partnerships with regional businesses in the new market. Using the partner's current client base and distribution channels, you can utilize their existing customer base and expertise while sharing risks and resources.

Direct Investment: Open branches, subsidiaries, or manufacturing facilities to create a physical presence in the new market. More control over operations, distribution, and customer connections is possible with this technique, but it does come with a high cost and a need for local market expertise.

8.3.3 Challenging the Dynamics of Local Markets

It is necessary to adjust to the distinct dynamics and preferences of the local market while entering new markets. The following things to keep in mind are:

Language and Cultural Differences: Recognize the language and cultural quirks of the new market. Make sure that your product offers, branding, and marketing messaging are appropriate for the local market. Think of collaborating with regional partners who are well-versed in the industry or employing local expertise.

Pricing and Payment Options: Modify your pricing plan to take into account the state of the local economy, consumer spending capacity, and competitive pricing. To ensure easy transactions, think about using local currencies and payment options.

Distribution and Logistics: Assess the infrastructure for local distribution channels and logistics. Find the most economical and efficient ways to provide your clients with your goods or services. To improve efficiency, think about collaborating with regional logistics companies or wholesalers.

Regulatory and Legal Compliance: Learn about the laws, ordinances, and requirements for obtaining a license in your area. Make sure that all local regulations pertaining to employment practices, data protection, intellectual property, and product safety are followed.

8.3.4 Promotion and Marketing in Emerging Markets

You must have strong marketing and promotion plans if you want to grow into new markets. Here are some crucial things to remember:

Localized marketing refers to creating advertising campaigns, promotional materials, and marketing messages that are specifically tailored to appeal to the local audience. For efficient communication, take linguistic preferences, cultural sensitivity, and local media outlets into account.

Digital marketing: To reach your target audience in the new market, make use of digital marketing channels including search engine optimization (SEO), social media marketing, and online advertising. Create regionalized websites and social media accounts to interact with clients.

Collaborations and Influencer Marketing: To boost brand awareness and credibility in the new market, work with like-minded local companies, industry insiders, or influencers. To increase brand recognition, look for collaborations with nearby businesses or provide sponsorships for events.

Customer connection management: Through individualized communication, top-notch customer support, and after-sales assistance, cultivate strong ties with clients in the new market. Gather customer feedback, respond to their issues, and modify your products in accordance with their preferences.

Entering new markets presents a stimulating prospect for expansion and diversity. You may successfully expand your firm and open up new opportunities for success by carrying out in-depth market research, creating a market entry plan, adjusting to local market characteristics, and putting effective marketing techniques into practice. Accept the difficulties and take advantage of the chances that come with branching out into new markets, and see your empire grow.

8.4 Overcoming Obstacles to Growth

When your company starts to grow exponentially, you need to be ready for the obstacles that come with that. Managing development can be exhilarating as well as intimidating, but you can overcome these obstacles if you have the correct techniques and frame of mind. This section will examine some of the typical growth obstacles that business owners encounter and go over good management techniques.

8.4.1 Supply and Demand Stabilization

A major obstacle that comes with expansion is the requirement to maintain a balance between supply and demand. It's critical to make sure you have adequate inventory, production capacity, and labor as your company grows in order to fulfill the rising demand from clients. If you don't, you risk missing out on chances, having unhappy consumers, and harming the reputation of your company.

It's critical to routinely evaluate your production and supply chain procedures in order to effectively handle this difficulty. Find any inefficiencies or bottlenecks that could make it more difficult for you to satisfy demand. To improve efficiency and production, think about using lean manufacturing concepts or utilizing technological solutions. To guarantee a consistent supply of resources, forge close ties with suppliers and look into outsourcing or joint venture opportunities.

8.4.2 Preserving Excellence and Client Contentment

It can get harder to keep up the same level of quality and client satisfaction as your firm expands. Making sure your goods and services still live up to the expectations of your target market is vital when you have more clients and more demand. If you don't, you risk losing customers, getting bad feedback, and harming the reputation of your company.

Give priority to client input and quality control in order to handle this difficulty. Put in place strong quality control procedures to guarantee that your goods and services constantly fulfill or surpass client expectations. Get input from your clients on a regular basis and utilize it to pinpoint areas that need work. Make an investment in your staff's training and development to provide them with the know-how and abilities needed to provide first-rate customer service. You can keep up a solid reputation and draw in new business by prioritizing quality and client happiness.

8.4.3 Infrastructure and Operational Scaling

Scaling your operations and infrastructure to meet the growing demand is crucial as your organization expands. This entails increasing your physical area, bringing up your technological setup, and bringing on more employees. On the other hand, growing too quickly or without enough preparation might result in operational difficulties, higher expenses, and inefficiencies.

Use a systematic way to scale your business efficiently. Examine your present activities in detail and note any areas that require development or improvement. Create a thorough plan that explains the actions and materials needed to grow your company. Think about making an investment in technological solutions that can boost productivity by automating procedures. When recruiting new staff members, give special attention to selecting people who share the same values as your business and possess the training and expertise needed to advance it. You may reduce interruptions and guarantee a seamless transition by approaching scalability with consideration and strategic planning.

8.4.4 Cash Flow Management

Effective cash flow management becomes more crucial as your company expands. You need to make sure you have enough working capital to fund your operations and that you have a clear grasp of your cash flow because of rising costs, rising inventory, and maybe longer payment cycles.

Create a thorough financial plan with estimated income and spending to manage cash flow efficiently. Keep a close eye on your financial flow to spot any possible problems or gaps. To close any cash flow gaps, think about putting tactics in place like negotiating advantageous payment terms with suppliers, providing incentives for early customer payment, or looking into financing options. Additionally, to guarantee on-time payments and reduce the chance of cash flow disruptions, keep a laser-like focus on controlling your accounts payable and receivable.

8.4.5 Changing with the Dynamics of the Market
The dynamics of the market may shift as your company expands, bringing with it both new opportunities and challenges. To be competitive and keep expanding, it's critical to maintain your flexibility and adjust to these changes.

Keep up with changes in consumer tastes and industry trends to efficiently adjust to shifting market conditions. Do market research on a regular basis to find new prospects and possible dangers. Encourage the innovative thinking of your staff and cultivate an innovative culture within the company. To keep one step ahead of the competition, be willing to try out novel tactics. You can set up your company for long-term success and growth by accepting change and being flexible.

Handling growth challenges is a continual process that calls for constant assessment, modification, and education. Through proactive, strategic, and customer-focused approaches, you may effectively manage these obstacles and sustain the expansion of your enterprise for rapid growth. Recall that development is an exciting adventure and that you can create a successful empire out of your entrepreneurial vision if you have the correct mindset and tactics.

NAVIGATING LEGAL AND REGULATORY CONSIDERATIONS

9.1 Knowledge of Business Rules and Laws

It is imperative for entrepreneurs to possess a comprehensive comprehension of the legal and regulatory environment in which their businesses function. In order to guarantee compliance, safeguard your intellectual property, control legal risks, and preserve the integrity of your contracts, you must be able to navigate the complicated world of business rules and regulations. The main business laws and regulations that each and every entrepreneur should be aware of are covered in this section.

9.1.1 The Value of Adherence

Following business laws and regulations is essential to operating a profitable and morally driven company, as well as being required by law. You may show that you are dedicated to upholding the rights of your stakeholders and conducting business with integrity by following the laws and rules that regulate your sector. Serious repercussions from noncompliance can include penalties, legal issues, harm to your company's reputation, and possibly even the closing of your doors.

It is crucial to keep up with the laws and rules that are relevant to your sector and area in order to assure compliance. This could entail speaking with legal experts, going to seminars for the business, and staying current with regulatory body updates and pertinent publications. You may reduce the dangers of non-compliance and set up your company for long-term success by being proactive and knowledgeable.

9.1.2 Different Kinds of Business Laws and Rules

A vast range of topics are covered by business rules and regulations, which regulate several facets of your entrepreneurial journey. Among the crucial aspects to be mindful of are:

9.1.2.1 Laws Concerning Companies

Business entities' creation, management, and

dissolution are governed by corporate laws. The legal prerequisites for forming a corporation are outlined in these statutes, together with information on shareholder agreements, corporate governance, and the registration procedure. Comprehending corporate laws is crucial to properly forming your company and guaranteeing adherence to transparency and reporting requirements.

9.1.2.2 Laws Concerning Employment

The relationship between employers and employees is governed by employment laws. These laws address things like discrimination, termination procedures, workplace safety, employee rights, and hiring practices. Maintaining a fair and inclusive workplace culture and averting legal conflicts with your staff members depend on your compliance with employment regulations.

Intellectual Property Laws 9.1.2.3

Trade secrets, patents, copyrights, and trademarks are examples of intangible assets that are protected by intellectual property laws. It is crucial to comprehend these regulations if you want to protect your original concepts, creations, and brand identification. You can stop someone from exploiting or making money off of your creations without your consent by protecting your intellectual property rights.

9.1.2.4 Laws Protecting Consumers

The purpose of consumer protection laws is

to safeguard customers against dishonest or fraudulent company practices. These rules control things like price, advertising, warranties, product labeling, and customer privacy. Maintaining a positive reputation and gaining the trust of your customers depend heavily on your adherence to consumer protection rules.

9.1.2.5 Laws Concerning Taxes

Businesses and individuals must comply with tax rules in order to pay their taxes. Maintaining compliance and avoiding fines requires that you comprehend your tax responsibilities, including payroll, sales, and income taxes. To guarantee proper and timely tax filings, it is advisable to speak with tax experts.

9.1.3 Getting Legal Advice

It can be difficult to navigate the complexities of company rules and regulations, particularly for entrepreneurs who do not have a background in law. Consulting with seasoned legal experts can guarantee that you are acting within the law's bounds and offer priceless advice.

When choosing a lawyer, seek out attorneys who specialize in business and entrepreneurship law. They may assist you in protecting your intellectual property, drafting and reviewing contracts, understanding the particular laws and rules that apply to your business, and providing advice on compliance-related issues. Developing a solid rapport with reliable legal counsel will ease your mind and support you in handling legal difficulties.

9.1.4 Keeping Current and Adjusting

Over time, changes and evolutions may occur in business rules and regulations. It is imperative to remain informed about any new laws or regulatory changes that could affect your company. This can be accomplished through attending legal seminars, subscribing to trade publications, and keeping in touch with attorneys on a regular basis.

Maintaining compliance and staying ahead of any legal problems require being able to adjust to changes in corporate laws and regulations. Ensuring the long-term profitability of your company and preventing legal problems can be achieved by periodically examining and upgrading your business procedures and policies to comply with current legal standards.

In summary

Being aware of company rules and regulations is essential to being an entrepreneur. You can manage legal risks, preserve the integrity of your contracts, safeguard your intellectual property, and traverse the complexity of compliance by being informed about the law, getting legal advice when necessary, and keeping up with any changes. You may establish a solid business foundation and put yourself in a position for long-term success by conducting business within the bounds of the law.

9.2 Intellectual Property Protection

For each entrepreneur, intellectual property (IP) is a vital resource. It includes mental works of art, inventions, designs, and brand names, among other intangible creations. Maintaining your competitive edge and making sure your company succeeds in the long run depend on protecting your intellectual property. This section will discuss the various forms of intellectual property, how important it is to protect them, and methods you may use to keep your works protected.

9.2.1 Comprehending Intellectual Property

There are four primary categories of intellectual property: trade secrets, copyrights, trademarks, and patents. Every variety has a unique function and offers various levels of security.

Patents: A patent is a legally recognized document that gives an inventor the sole right to use their innovation. It offers defense for novel and practical devices, compositions of matter, processes, and advancements therein. With a patent, an inventor has the temporary right to stop others from creating, utilizing, importing, selling, or importing their creation without their consent.

Brands

Trademarks are unique symbols, signs, or emblems that set one company's products or services apart from another. They may include taglines, brand names, or even particular hues or noises. Through trademark protection, third parties are prevented from utilizing marks that are confusing to consumers and harm a brand's reputation.

Copyright protection

Original works of authorship, such as plays, songs, artwork, and books, are safeguarded by copyright laws. They grant the author the only authority to make copies, give them away, exhibit, perform, and alter their creations. Copyright protection is automatically granted at the time of creation and is valid for the duration of the author's life plus an extra year.

Trade Secrets

Trade secrets are valuable and sensitive commercial information that provides a business with a competitive edge. Formulas, procedures, client lists, and marketing plans are a few examples of this. In contrast to copyrights, patents, and trademarks, trade secrets are not registered with the public. Rather, they are safeguarded by security protocols and confidentiality agreements.

9.2.2 The Value of Intellectual Property Protection
It is imperative that you safeguard your intellectual property for multiple reasons.

Maintaining a competitive edge
You can gain a competitive edge in the market by preventing others from utilizing or copying your creations by protecting your intellectual property. Maintaining your unique selling proposition and setting yourself apart from the competition are made possible by it.

Increasing the Value of a Brand
Trademarks and copyrights are examples of intellectual property that add to the total value of your brand. It fosters consumer trust, loyalty, and brand recognition. By keeping your brand assets unique to your company, you can preserve its worth and reputation.

Creating Income
Selling or licensing intellectual property are two ways to make money off of it. By allowing others permission to use your intellectual property in exchange for royalties or other fees, you can create additional cash streams by safeguarding your inventions.

Avoiding unauthorized utilization
Your intellectual property is susceptible to infringement if it is not properly protected.

Unauthorized use of your works may result in a loss of market share, financial losses, and harm to the reputation of your brand. By safeguarding your intellectual property, you can assert your legal rights and prosecute infringers.

9.2.3 Methods of Intellectual Property Protection
To protect your intellectual property, think about putting the following tactics into practice:

Perform an entire intellectual property assessment.
Make an inventory of your intellectual property assets first. List all of the works—inventions, designs, logos, textual materials, etc.—that might be protected. To prioritize your protection efforts, evaluate each asset's potential dangers and worth.

Register for Copyrights, Trademarks, and Patents
To obtain exclusive rights for inventions or novel processes, think about submitting a patent application. To make sure your innovation satisfies the requirements and to successfully navigate the challenging application procedure, collaborate with a patent attorney. File for copyright protection for your creative works and trademark protection for your brand's assets.

Put confidentiality measures in place.
Establish stringent confidentiality procedures for trade secrets and private company data. When disclosing confidential information to contractors, workers, or prospective partners, use

non-disclosure agreements (NDAs). Implement safe systems for communication and storage, and restrict access to sensitive information.

Keep an eye on and defend your rights.
Keep an eye out for any intellectual property infringements on the market on a regular basis. Search the internet, keep an eye on what your competitors are doing, and hire experts to find any unauthorized use. If an infringement is found, seek the proper remedies and safeguard your rights by filing a lawsuit as soon as possible.

Teach Your Group
Make certain that the members of your team and staff are aware of the value of protecting intellectual property. Teach them how to use copyrights and trademarks, handle private information with care, and report any possible infringements. Encourage your company to have an intellectual property-friendly culture.

Consult a lawyer.
Laws pertaining to intellectual property can be complicated and differ between states. It is wise to consult a knowledgeable intellectual property lawyer with experience in the area in question. They can support you through the process of safeguarding your intellectual property and assist you in resolving any potential legal issues.

In summary
Preserving your competitive edge, building brand

equity, and stopping the illegal exploitation of your inventions are all dependent on protecting your intellectual property. Understanding the various forms of intellectual property and putting the right plans into action can help you protect your priceless assets and make sure your company succeeds in the long run. Recall that maintaining intellectual property protection is a continuous process that calls for alertness and preemptive action to keep up with the ever-changing business environment.

9.3 Fulfilling Tax Liabilities

It is crucial for an entrepreneur to comprehend and honor their tax obligations. Any economy must have taxes in order to run, and breaking the tax code can have dire repercussions for your company. This section will discuss the significance of meeting tax responsibilities and offer helpful advice on navigating the tricky terrain of business taxes.

9.3.1 Getting to Know Business Taxes

It is essential to grasp the various tax types that could be applicable to your company before delving into the finer points of tax compliance. The following are some typical corporate tax types:

Income Tax: This tax is imposed on the money that your company makes. Depending on your company's legal structure—sole proprietorship, partnership, or corporation, for example—the tax rate may change.

Sales Tax: A tax levied on the exchange of products and services is known as a sales tax. Each jurisdiction has its own sales tax rate and set of rules, so it's important to know what the particular needs are in your area.

Payroll Tax: In the event that you have workers, you will be in charge of deducting and sending in payroll taxes, which consist of Medicare, Social Security, and federal and state income taxes.

Property Tax: Your business's personal and real estate holdings, including buildings, machinery, and land, are subject to property taxation based on their respective values.

Excise Tax: Excise taxes are levied on particular products or activities, such as cigarettes, alcohol, fuel, and particular kinds of services.

Estimated Tax: In order to avoid fines, you might

need to make estimated tax payments throughout the year if your company is anticipated to owe a sizable amount of tax at the end of the year.

9.3.2 Getting Expert Counsel

It can be difficult to navigate the complexities of tax regulations, particularly if you are not familiar with the nuances of corporate taxation. Getting expert guidance from a licensed tax accountant or tax lawyer is strongly advised. These experts can assist you in comprehending your particular tax responsibilities, locating possible credits and deductions, and making sure you are in conformity with all relevant tax regulations.

Establishing an effective record-keeping system to monitor your income, expenses, and other financial transactions can also be helped by a tax expert. In addition to making tax filing simpler, this will provide you with important information on the state of your company's finances.

9.3.3 Getting a Tax Identification Number Registered

It is imperative that you receive the required tax identification numbers in order to fulfill your tax obligations. In the US, the following tax identification numbers are most frequently used by businesses:

Employer Identification Number (EIN): The Internal Revenue Service (IRS) assigns an EIN, a distinct nine-digit number, to your company in order to identify it for tax purposes. If you meet certain requirements, operate as a company or partnership, or have workers, you will require an EIN.

Sales Tax Permit: You might be required to apply for a sales tax permit from your state's tax authority if your company offers taxable products or services. You are able to collect and submit sales tax on behalf of the state with this permit.

State Employer Identification Number: In order to file state taxes, several states require that companies get a unique employer identification number. If you're unsure if this is required for your business, check with the tax authority in your state.

Obtaining extra tax identification numbers, such as a federal excise tax number or a state-specific tax identification number, may be necessary, depending on the type of business you operate.

9.3.4 Keeping Correct Financial Documents
To ensure tax compliance, financial documents must be kept up-to-date and well organized. Maintaining meticulous records of all your business's earnings, outlays, and other financial dealings is vital. The following are some guidelines for keeping correct financial records:

Keep Your Personal and Business Finances Apart: Create a separate bank account for your company and utilize it just for business-related transactions. This will ensure that you are not combining your personal and business funds, and it will make it simpler to track your revenue and expenses for your firm.

Employ Accounting Software: To make your financial record-keeping procedure more efficient, think about utilizing accounting software. You may streamline tax preparation, create financial statements, and keep track of your income and expenses with the aid of these tools.

Save Invoices and Receipts: Save all invoices, receipts, and other supporting documentation related to your business spending. These records show what you've spent and can support any deductions you make on your tax return.

Track Mileage: Maintain a record of your mileage if you drive a car for work. You can use this to figure out how much your car expenses will be after the deductible.

Keep Your Records Organized: Establish a strategy for keeping your financial documents organized, whether they are on your computer or in physical folders. Store all pertinent documents in a location that is both secure and convenient.

9.3.5 Tax Return and Payment

One ongoing duty for business owners is to file and pay taxes. Depending on the kind of tax and your jurisdiction, there will be different dates and criteria. The following general rules should be remembered:

Income Tax: An annual income tax return must be filed by the majority of enterprises. Generally, you have until April 15th to file your return, although this can change based on your company's legal structure. For the most recent information, see the IRS guidelines or speak with a tax professional.

Sales Tax: If your company is obliged to collect sales tax, you will have to submit sales tax returns on a regular basis and send the money you collect to the relevant tax authorities. Your jurisdiction will determine how frequently you file and how much you have to pay.

Payroll Tax: If you have employees, you must regularly remit payroll taxes to the relevant tax authorities by withholding them from their paychecks. The size of your payroll as well as the regulations of state and federal tax authorities will determine how frequently you must deposit payroll taxes.

Estimated Tax: You might have to pay estimated taxes all year if your company is anticipated to owe a sizable sum of money in taxes at the end of the year. Usually, these payments are due on a quarterly basis.

It's critical to keep up with any modifications to tax laws and rules that could have an impact on your company. For the most recent information, speak with a tax professional or use reliable resources like the IRS website.

9.3.6 Steer clear of audits and tax penalties.
Tax duties that are not followed may result in penalties, fines, and even legal repercussions. Here are some pointers to remember in order to prevent these problems:

File and settle on time: Ensure that you submit your tax returns and settle any outstanding balances by the dates given by the relevant taxing authorities. Interest and penalties may apply for late filings or payments.

Precise Reporting: Verify that all the data you have included on your tax filings is precise and comprehensive. An audit and possible penalties may result from inaccurate reporting.

Honesty and Transparency: When filing your taxes, act with integrity and transparency. Refrain from committing fraud, trying to conceal income, or inflating deductions.

Keep Records: Save all of the paperwork you need to support your tax returns, such as invoices, financial statements, and receipts. In the case of an audit, requests for certain papers may be made.

Seek specialist advice: Consult a specialist if you have any questions regarding any element of your tax duties. You may make sure you are in compliance and manage the complexities of tax regulations with the assistance of a tax professional.

Recall that paying taxes is not merely required by law but also by morality. You support public services and infrastructure and contribute to the smooth operation of society by paying your taxes.

In summary

Keeping up with tax duties is crucial to operating a profitable and moral corporation. You may make sure that your company complies with tax rules by learning about the various tax types, getting professional assistance, registering for the required tax identification numbers, keeping proper financial records, and filing and paying taxes on time. In addition to avoiding fines and other legal repercussions, paying your taxes on time also improves society as a whole.

9.4 Handling Contracts and Legal Risks

It is essential for entrepreneurs to comprehend and control the legal risks involved in operating a business. For your business to be protected and successful in the long run, you must navigate the legal landscape, from contracts to regulatory compliance. In this part, we will go over the most important things to think about while handling contracts and legal issues as a business.

9.4.1 Recognizing Legal Hazards

Operating a business entails legal risks that, if not effectively managed, can have serious repercussions. You can reduce these hazards by being aware of them and taking preventative action. The following are some typical legal risks that business owners need to be mindful of:

Contractual Hazards

Any business connection is built on contracts, so it's important to comprehend their terms and restrictions. Contractual duties that are not met may give rise to litigation and financial consequences. Contracts must be properly reviewed and negotiated to guarantee that they serve your interests and your company's goals.

Risks Associated with Intellectual Property

For many businesses, intellectual property (IP) is a valued asset. It's crucial to safeguard your intellectual property (IP) with trade secrets, copyrights, patents, and trademarks to stop others from utilizing or making money off of your inventions. Intellectual property infringement and loss of competitive advantage might result from failing to protect your work.

Risks Associated with Compliance

Maintaining legal and regulatory compliance is essential to operating a business. Penalties, fines, and reputational harm may arise from noncompliance. Maintaining current knowledge of pertinent laws and regulations, as well as putting procedures in place to guarantee compliance, is crucial when it comes to matters like data security, employment legislation, and industry-specific requirements.

Risks Associated with Liability

Product liability, professional liability, and premises liability are just a few of the potential concerns that entrepreneurs may encounter. It is imperative for businesses to comprehend and mitigate these risks by implementing suitable insurance policies and risk management techniques in order to safeguard against monetary damages and litigation.

9.4.2 Administration of Contracts

Contracts are legally binding agreements that specify each party's rights and responsibilities. Securing efficient business operations and reducing legal risks require effective contract administration. In order to manage contracts, keep the following points in mind:

Simple and direct language

In order to prevent ambiguity and misinterpretation, contracts should be written in clear and straightforward language. Give each party a clear definition of their rights and obligations, including information about deliverables, deadlines, payment terms, and dispute resolution procedures.

Consult a lawyer.
When drafting or revising contracts, it is strongly advised to have legal counsel. A knowledgeable lawyer can assist in making sure your contracts are compliant with applicable laws and regulations, safeguard your interests, and are legally sound.

Examine and bargain.
Before signing any contracts, carefully go through and negotiate them. Keep an eye out for important elements, including liability limitations, indemnity agreements, and termination clauses. Strive to reach a reasonable compromise between the parties and negotiate conditions that will benefit your business.

Maintaining Records
Keep a thorough record of every contract, including signed copies, negotiation-related communications, and modifications. When it comes to conflicts or legal matters, this material can be extremely helpful.

9.4.3 Adherence to the Law
Adherence to legal statutes and regulations is vital for the enduring prosperity and durability of your enterprise. In order to manage legal compliance,

keep the following points in mind:

Keep up with it.
Keep abreast of the laws and rules that are pertinent to your business and sector. To guarantee continued compliance, evaluate legal requirements on a regular basis and consult a specialist.

Create guidelines and protocols.
Create and put into effect policies and processes that comply with the law. These could include employment rules, health and safety procedures, and data protection regulations. Review and update these rules frequently to take into account modifications to laws and regulations.

Instruction and Training
Make sure your staff members are informed and trained in legal compliance. By doing this, you can make sure that everyone in your company is aware of their roles and how crucial it is to follow the law.

Keep an eye on and audit
Keep a close eye on and audit your company's operations to spot any compliance lapses or possible threats. To guarantee continued compliance, carry out internal audits and, if needed, consult outside experts.

9.4.4 Handling Legal Conflicts
Even with the best of intentions, operating a business can lead to legal difficulties. Here are some important things to think about when

handling legal disputes:

Dispute Resolution Through Alternative Methods
Think about using alternative conflict resolution procedures like arbitration or mediation as a quick and affordable approach to settling disagreements. These techniques can assist in maintaining corporate partnerships and preventing drawn-out, expensive legal disputes.

Legal Assistance
In the event that a legal disagreement emerges, get advice from an accomplished lawyer who focuses on the pertinent legal topic. You can safeguard your interests and be guided through the dispute resolution procedure by a knowledgeable lawyer.

Record and maintain proof.
Keep track of and document all pertinent evidence pertaining to the disagreement. Contracts, letters, bills, and any other paperwork that bolsters your argument can be included here.

Settlement and Negotiation
Investigate your choices for settlement and negotiation to end the conflict peacefully. Find a solution that benefits both parties by having an honest and constructive conversation.

The final option is litigation.
When every other course of action has been taken, litigation ought to be the final one. The process of litigation can be costly, time-consuming, and unpredictable. To safeguard your rights and

interests, nevertheless, might be important in specific circumstances.

Understanding and controlling contractual and legal risks can help you safeguard your company, reduce liabilities, and maintain legal and regulatory compliance. To properly manage legal considerations, establish strong procedures and, when necessary, seek professional counsel. You'll be well-prepared to handle the legal system and concentrate on expanding your business empire if you accomplish this.

BUILDING STRATEGIC PARTNERSHIPS AND ALLIANCES

10.1 Finding Possible Affiliates

Alliances and partnerships can be effective instruments for business owners trying to expand. You can reach a wider audience, obtain more resources, and take advantage of complementary skills by working with other companies or people. But not all relationships are made equal; therefore, it's critical to find the ideal possible mate for your unique requirements and objectives. We will look at methods in this section for finding compatible people and making the most of these connections.

10.1.1 Outlining the Goals of Your Partnership

It's critical to have a clear idea of your partnership objectives before you start looking for possible partners. What do you want a partnership to accomplish? Are you trying to improve your product offering, get access to new distribution channels, or increase the size of your consumer base? You may focus your search and identify partners who share your goals by establishing your objectives.

10.1.2 Looking into Possible Partners

It's time to begin your partner investigation when you have established your partnership goals. Start by figuring out who or what kinds of businesses are involved in your target market or industry. Seek out businesses that cater to a similar clientele or that provide complimentary goods or services. When assessing possible partners, take reputation, market presence, and financial soundness into account.

To learn more about possible partners, consult trade journals, professional networks, and internet resources. Seek out businesses with a history of fruitful alliances and a standing for cooperation. To make sure that their beliefs, culture, and strategic direction coincide with your own company, pay close attention to these factors.

10.1.3 Creating Connections and Networking
Finding possible partners through networking is a very effective strategy. To meet business owners and experts who share your interests, go to trade exhibits, conferences, and networking events. Take part in discussions, share ideas, and look into possible joint ventures. Developing connections with people and businesses in your sector might lead to beneficial alliances.

Use social media and internet resources in addition to in-person networking to grow your network. Participate in online debates, join industry-specific organizations and forums, and establish connections with experts who have similar interests. Use these channels to interact with possible partners, showcasing your knowledge and enthusiasm for working together.

10.1.4 Assessing Possible Affiliates
It's critical to assess a possible partner's suitability

for a relationship once you've located them and made the initial introductions. Think about things like their reputation, resources, and level of experience. Examine their past performance in forming effective alliances and their reliability in keeping their word.

Assess how well your organizations align with one another's values, culture, and strategic direction. A relationship ought to benefit both parties and be based on mutual respect and objectives. Seek partners who will help you accomplish your goals by providing resources and abilities that complement your own.

10.1.5 Reaching and Forming Agreements
It's time to discuss and set up the partnership when you have found a possible partner and assessed their suitability. Clearly state each party's expectations as well as their duties and obligations. Provide a structure for communicating, making decisions, and resolving disputes.

Think about the partnership's financial and legal components, such as ownership, profit-sharing, and intellectual property rights. To make sure that the partnership agreement safeguards each party's interests and reduces any potential dangers, get legal counsel.

10.1.6 Working Together for Our Own Growth
The foundation of a good partnership is mutual

progress and cooperation. Work closely with your partner to maximize each other's resources and strengths once the relationship has been formed. Maintain open lines of communication and information sharing to guarantee alignment and optimize the partnership's value.

Examine possibilities for collaborative marketing campaigns, co-creation of goods or services, and cross-promotion. You may reach a larger audience and develop distinctive value propositions by pooling your resources and expertise.

10.1.7 Keeping and Developing Connections

Developing a great collaboration takes constant work and care; it doesn't happen overnight. Evaluate the partnership's development on a regular basis and make any improvements. Keep the lines of communication open and respond quickly to any problems or complaints.

Make an effort to cultivate enduring bonds with your significant others. Together, celebrate accomplishments, give credit where credit is due, and express gratitude for the support received. By fostering the relationship, you may lay the groundwork for ongoing cooperation and development on both sides.

To sum up, finding possible partners is an essential first step in creating strategic alliances that might advance your company. Finding the ideal partners who share your objectives and values can be achieved by clearly outlining your partnership's goals, carrying out an in-depth investigation, networking, and assessing possible partners. You may take advantage of these collaborations to promote success and mutual progress by collaborating skillfully, negotiating, and managing your relationships.

10.2 Partnership Negotiation and Structure

Entrepreneurs who want to build their companies and access new markets may find that partnerships are an effective tool. You can reach new markets, obtain more resources, and benefit from your partners' knowledge by working together with other people or companies. On the other hand, partnership negotiations and structuring can be difficult procedures that require considerable thought and preparation. In this section, we'll go over the essential processes for building and negotiating partnerships and provide you with useful advice for making the most of your teamwork.

10.2.1 Finding Possible Affiliates

Finding possible partners that share your values and company objectives is crucial before you start the partnership negotiation process. When assessing possible mates, take into account the following factors:

Finding a partner with complementary talents and knowledge might help you achieve your goals. This can help close any knowledge gaps you may have and improve your partnership's overall potential.

Similar Vision and Values: Finding partners who have comparable vision and values is essential. This alignment will guarantee that you are working toward shared objectives and facilitate overcoming any obstacles that may come up.

Reputation and Performance History: Examine prospective partners' performance histories and reputations. Seek partners with a solid industry reputation and a track record of accomplishment.

Network and Connections: Take into account the connections and network that possible partners may offer. A good network partner can help you reach a wider audience and open doors to new opportunities.

10.2.2 Agreeing to Terms of Partnership

The next stage is to discuss the partnership's

conditions when you have found possible partners. This entails talking over and deciding on a number of collaboration-related issues, such as:

Goals and Objectives: Clearly state the partnership's aims and objectives. This will make it easier to make sure that everyone is working toward the same goals and is aware of what those goals are.

Functions and Accountabilities: Establish the functions and accountability of every collaborator. Give specific instructions on who will be in charge of what and how choices will be made.

Resource Distribution: Talk about how the partners will divide up resources, including cash, people, and gear. To make sure the partnership succeeds, it is crucial to distribute resources fairly and equally.

Timeline and Milestones: Define a schedule for the collaboration and assign due dates to monitor advancement. This will guarantee that everyone is held responsible and that the collaboration is progressing according to schedule.

Risk and Liability: Talk about the partnership's possible risks and liabilities. Establish a plan for managing these risks, and assign blame for any possible losses or harm.

Exit Strategy: In the event that the collaboration does not turn out as expected, it is critical to have a plan on how to end it. Talk about the possible ways to end the collaboration or make changes if needed.

10.2.3 Putting the Partnership in Order

The partnership needs to be structured when the agreements have been agreed upon. There are numerous kinds of partnerships to take into account, such as:

General Partnership: All partners in a general partnership are equally liable and responsible for the company. This kind of collaboration is very easy to establish and is frequently utilized by small companies.

Limited Partnership: General partners and limited partners make up a limited partnership. Limited partners have limited liability and are passive investors, whereas general partners have unlimited liability and actively participate in the day-to-day activities of the company.

A limited liability partnership (LLP) is a type of partnership where the liability of each partner is restricted. This implies that partners are not held individually liable for the partnership's obligations and liabilities.

Joint Venture: A joint venture is a company established for a particular goal or mission. Profits and losses are divided in accordance with the terms of the agreement, and each partner provides resources and experience to the business.

It is crucial to seek advice from legal and financial experts when forming a partnership to make sure you are selecting the best arrangement for your unique requirements.

10.2.4 Keeping and Developing Connections
It's critical to actively preserve and grow your relationship with your partners after it's been formed. The following advice can assist you in cultivating a fruitful partnership:

Communication: Keep lines of communication open and honest with your partners. Provide them with regular updates on the partnership's development and take care of any questions or problems that could come up.

Collaboration: Encourage an atmosphere of cooperation in which each partner feels important and involved. To get the most out of the collaboration, promote the exchange of knowledge and ideas.

Mutual Benefits: Make sure that both parties are getting benefits from the collaboration by regularly evaluating it. Review the partnership's aims and objectives on a regular basis and make any required revisions.

Conflict Resolution: To handle any disputes or conflicts that may occur, develop efficient conflict resolution techniques. It is critical to identify solutions that work for both parties and to address these difficulties as soon as possible.

Frequent Assessment: Conduct regular assessments of the collaboration to determine its efficacy and pinpoint areas in need of development. This can make sure that the collaboration keeps adding value and is in line with your company's objectives.

You may negotiate and create partnerships that will support the expansion and success of your company by using these processes and best practices. Recall that relationships are two-way and that you should put in time and effort to establish and preserve solid bonds with your partners.

10.3 Working Together for Our Own Growth

Working together is an effective strategy that can take your company to new heights. You may access new markets, more resources, and the knowledge of others by establishing strategic alliances and partnerships. This section will discuss the value of working together for growth on both sides and offer doable tactics for creating enduring alliances.

10.3.1 The Advantages of Teamwork

For business owners aiming to expand, teamwork provides a host of advantages. Here are a few main benefits:

Getting to Know New Clients and Markets

You can enter new markets and have access to their consumer base by forming partnerships with other companies. Compared to working alone, this can help you develop your consumer base and boost sales more quickly.

Pooled Resources and Knowledge
You can combine resources and skills with your partners when you collaborate. This can involve pooling both intellectual and physical resources, such as knowledge and abilities, as well as resources like office space and equipment. You can do more as a team than you could alone by utilizing each other's strengths.

Mitigation of Risk
Working together with other companies allows you to split the risks involved in taking on new tasks or endeavors. This can raise the chances of success and lessen the financial burden. You can lessen the impact of possible failures by distributing the risk among several parties.

Creativity and innovation
Innovation and fresh ideas are frequently produced through collaboration. Bringing people together who have different experiences and viewpoints can help to promote creativity and unconventional thinking. This may lead to the creation of distinctive goods or services that distinguish you from rivals.

10.3.2 Selecting the Appropriate Partners

Selecting the appropriate partners is essential to a fruitful working relationship. The following steps will assist you in finding possible partners:

Establish your goals.
Prior to looking for partners, it's critical to specify your goals and the outcomes you want from the partnership. This will assist you in finding collaborators who share your objectives and can support your expansion plan.

Examine the market.
Find possible partners by conducting in-depth market research to find companies that operate in adjacent or complementary industries. Seek out companies that target comparable clientele, have comparable values, or provide complementary goods or services to your own.

Make connections and go to industry events.
One useful method for locating possible partners is networking. Attend trade fairs, conferences, and industry events to network with other like-minded business owners and discover potential joint ventures. Talk to them, share ideas, and cultivate a friendship with someone who might become your partner.

Make use of Internet resources.
Make use of internet groups and platforms to establish connections with possible partners. Businesses willing to work together can be found through social media groups, industry-specific

forums, and websites like LinkedIn.

10.3.3 Creating Effective Collaborations
Once possible partners have been found, it's critical to set up your collaborations to support success and growth for both parties. Here are some crucial things to remember:

Define roles and responsibilities clearly.
Give each member of the partnership a clear understanding of their roles and responsibilities. This will guarantee that there is no misunderstanding and that each person is aware of their own responsibilities and contributions.

Clarify your expectations and goals.
Establish precise objectives and standards for the collaboration. This entails stating your shared objectives, the timetable for accomplishing them, and the success indicators. Review and reevaluate these objectives on a regular basis to make sure the collaboration stays in line with your overarching business plan.

Create efficient channels of communication.
Successful teamwork requires honest and efficient communication. Establish regular avenues for communication, like meetings that happen once a week or once a month, to talk about progress, resolve issues, and make decisions. To promote trust and openness, all parties should communicate in an honest and open manner.

Create a Mutual Benefits Contract.

Draft a legal agreement outlining the partnership's terms and conditions. The parameters of the partnership, each partner's obligations, how resources and earnings will be shared, as well as any exit plans or dispute resolution procedures, should all be spelled out in this agreement. When creating such agreements, it is advisable to consult a lawyer to make sure all parties are covered.

10.3.4 Developing and Sustaining Connections
Developing strong relationships takes constant work and care; it is not a one-time thing. The following are some tactics to preserve and strengthen your working relationships:

Encourage openness and trust.
Any effective partnership is built on trust. Communicate openly, follow through on your promises, and behave with integrity. Although it takes time to develop confidence, it is crucial for sustained cooperation.

Periodically assess and modify
Review your partnerships' growth and efficacy on a regular basis. Evaluate whether the partnership is helping you achieve your goals and whether any changes need to be made. This could entail going over the objectives again, clarifying roles and duties, or looking into potential new growth areas.

Honor accomplishments and draw lessons from mistakes.
Celebrate and recognize the accomplishments

made possible by teamwork. Acknowledge each partner's input and thank them for their work. Apply the same principle to failures and setbacks. Take advantage of them as chances for development and progress, and cooperate to overcome obstacles.

Keep the lines of communication open.
Keep in constant contact with your partners to learn about their needs, difficulties, and opportunities. Share information, opinions, and updates on a regular basis to promote teamwork. Promote open communication and show openness to thoughts and comments from each partner.

In summary
Working together is a great way to succeed and grow as a team. Through the establishment of strategic partnerships and alliances, business owners can gain access to new markets, extra resources, and the knowledge of others. Identifying compatible partners, establishing prosperous alliances, and cultivating cooperative connections are essential measures for optimizing the advantages of cooperation. Accept the potential of teamwork to create new avenues for the development and growth of your company.

10.4 Sustaining and Developing Connections

Creating strategic alliances and partnerships is essential to expanding a successful company. But once the alliance is formed, the labor doesn't stop. It is crucial to sustain and grow these relationships over time if you want to get the most out of them. This section will discuss how important it is to maintain relationships with your partners and offer tips on how to do so for long-term success.

10.4.1 Have regular communication.
Successful relationships are built on effective communication. Having honest and open lines of communication with your partners is crucial. Provide them with regular updates on the state of your company, pertinent information, and resolution of any issues or problems that may come up. Maintaining open channels of communication will help you fortify your relationship and develop trust.

10.4.2 Promote understanding amongst people
Fostering mutual understanding between you and your partners is essential to maintaining a happy and fruitful partnership. Spend some

time learning about their objectives, difficulties, and top concerns. This will enable you to coordinate your efforts and work toward common goals. Building a solid foundation for a long-lasting relationship can be achieved by exhibiting empathy and paying attention to what your partners have to say.

10.4.3 Offer something of worth.
Continually adding value to your partner's relationship is one of the finest methods to foster and preserve it. Seek out chances to encourage and help your partners reach their objectives. This might be lending a hand in areas where you are knowledgeable, giving access to resources, or exchanging industry ideas. You may develop a relationship that benefits both of you and cement the bond by actively supporting your partner's success.

10.4.4 Together, celebrate your accomplishments.
It's crucial to celebrate victories and milestones with your spouse when you both reach them. Acknowledge the contributions made by your partners and thank them for their assistance. Not only does celebrating accomplishments improve the relationship, but it also creates a cooperative and upbeat environment. It fosters a feeling of unity and supports ongoing development and achievement.

10.4.5 Proactively resolve disputes
Disagreements and conflicts will inevitably arise

in any kind of relationship, including business relationships. It's critical to resolve disagreements early on and in a positive way. Disagreements should not be allowed to linger and worsen because this can ruin the relationship. Instead, approach disagreements with an open mind, make an effort to comprehend the viewpoints of all sides, and endeavor to come up with a solution that works for everyone. You may maintain the integrity of the partnership by promptly and respectfully resolving issues.

10.4.6 Seek input for ongoing development.
You need to ask your partners for input if you want to keep and grow your relationship. Seek their feedback on a regular basis regarding the partnership's performance and potential areas for development. Pay attention to what they have to say, and make sure you take it into account when making judgments. You can establish a culture of growth and cooperation and show your commitment to the relationship by consistently asking for input and working toward improvement.

10.4.7 Periodically assess the collaboration.
It is essential to regularly assess the collaboration in order to guarantee its sustained success. Give the collaboration a thorough evaluation, note any areas that could be improved, and make the required changes. Together with your partners, you should have frank and open discussions

throughout this evaluation so that you can both assess your progress and make plans for the future. You can adjust to shifting conditions and make sure the partnership continues to be advantageous to both parties by routinely reviewing it.

10.4.8 Be flexible and adaptive.

Because business environments are ever-changing, it's critical to be flexible and adaptive in how you build and preserve relationships. Stay receptive to fresh perspectives and opportunities, and be prepared to modify your plans and strategy as necessary. Being adaptable helps you and your partners overcome obstacles and grab new chances, building stronger bonds in the process.

10.4.9 Make an investment in the bond.

Relationships need time, energy, and resources to be nurtured and maintained. Setting the connection as a top priority and allocating the funds required to foster its expansion and improvement are crucial. This could be setting aside time for frequent meetings, going to trade shows as a group, or funding cooperative marketing campaigns. You show your commitment to the relationship's success by making an investment in it.

10.4.10: Honor inclusivity and diversity.

Success in today's global corporate environment is largely determined by diversity and inclusivity. Recognize the distinct viewpoints and experiences that each of your partners brings to the table, and embrace and promote their variety. Encourage a welcoming atmosphere where everyone's opinions are respected and heard. One way to strengthen and fortify your partnership is to embrace diversity and inclusivity.

It takes commitment, communication, and understanding on both sides to uphold and nurture relationships with your partners. By implementing these tactics, you can create enduring alliances that support the expansion and prosperity of your company. Recall that investing in connections is crucial for long-term success, as they serve as the cornerstone of any successful endeavor.

ADAPTING TO CHANGE AND EMBRACING INNOVATION

11.1 Understanding the Necessity of Adjustment

Any entrepreneur who hopes to succeed in the long run must possess the ability to adapt to the fast-paced and constantly evolving business landscape of today. The first step in embracing change and innovation is realizing the need for adaptability, which is a skill that can be acquired and refined over time.

11.1.1 Adopting an Innovative Culture

Entrepreneurs must first foster an innovative culture within their companies in order to realize the need for adaptability. This entails creating an atmosphere that values innovation and creativity and views failure as a chance for personal development.

Innovation can take many different forms, such as creating new goods or services or figuring out how to run a company more profitably. Entrepreneurs can cultivate an environment where people are open to change and new chances by pushing staff members to think creatively and try out novel ideas.

11.1.2 Viewing Change as a Chance

In the business world, change is unavoidable; therefore, entrepreneurs need to learn to view it as an opportunity rather than a threat. Entrepreneurs may maintain a competitive edge and establish themselves as leaders in their field by embracing change.

Being proactive and always monitoring the company environment for new trends and changes in client preferences is necessary when recognizing the need for adaptation. This calls for entrepreneurs to be risk-takers and willing to venture outside of their comfort zones, as well as open-minded and willing to challenge the status quo.

11.1.3 Ongoing Enhancement
Acknowledging the necessity for adaptation necessitates a dedication to ongoing enhancement. This entails continuously assessing and improving company procedures, goods, and services to make sure they stay competitive and relevant.

To pinpoint areas that need improvement, entrepreneurs should often ask stakeholders, such as staff members and clients, for their opinions. Entrepreneurs can maintain their flexibility and responsiveness to shifting market conditions by adopting a philosophy of continual improvement.

11.1.4 Recognizing and Addressing Industry Upheavals
In the quickly changing corporate environment of today, industrial disruptions are happening increasingly frequently. To stay ahead of the curve, entrepreneurs need to be watchful and proactive in predicting and responding to these disruptions.

Being aware of market disruption-causing trends in the sector and new technology is essential to recognizing the need for adaptation. Through vigilant monitoring of the sector, entrepreneurs are able to spot possible risks and possibilities and modify their company plans in a preemptive manner.

In order to enable staff members to react swiftly to shifts in the market, entrepreneurs also need to cultivate an environment of agility and adaptability within their companies. To remain competitive, this can entail reviewing business plans, looking into new alliances, or even venturing into untapped markets.

In summary
To succeed in the fast-paced business world of today, entrepreneurs must possess the vital ability to adapt. Entrepreneurs can set themselves up for long-term success by embracing an innovative culture, viewing change as an opportunity, dedicating themselves to continuous improvement, and anticipating and reacting to disruptions in their market.

Rather than being a one-time occurrence, adaptation is a continuous process that calls for continued awareness and an openness to change. Entrepreneurs may reach their full potential and create successful, long-lasting empires by realizing the necessity for adaptation and acting proactively to stay ahead of the curve.

11.2 Adopting an Innovative Culture

In the ever-changing corporate environment of today, innovation is now essential for both survival and expansion, rather than a luxury. In order to maintain a competitive edge and achieve sustained prosperity, business owners need to encourage a culture of innovation in their establishments. This chapter will examine the value of embracing innovation, offer tactics for developing an innovative culture, and emphasize the advantages it can have for your company.

11.2.1 Innovation's Significance

The foundation of any successful company is innovation. It enables business owners to recognize fresh opportunities, adjust to shifting market conditions, and develop distinctive value propositions. Entrepreneurs may set themselves apart from rivals, draw in and keep clients, and promote long-term success by embracing innovation.

Innovation encompasses all facets of a business, including procedures, offerings, and corporate structures. It is not just restricted to product development. Entrepreneurs may streamline their processes, improve client experiences, and gain a competitive edge by consistently looking for new and innovative methods to innovate.

11.2.2 Methods for Fostering an Innovative Culture

Establishing an innovative culture calls for a methodical and purposeful strategy. The following tactics can assist you in encouraging creativity inside your company:

1. Promote and honor originality.

Establish an atmosphere that inspires staff members to express their thoughts and think creatively. Create avenues for the exchange of ideas and offer rewards for creativity. Acknowledge and thank staff members who offer creative fixes or recommendations.

2. Adopt a growth perspective.

Encourage a growth attitude in your company, wherein failure is viewed as a chance for development and learning. Encourage staff members to try new things, take measured risks, and learn from both successes and mistakes. Establish a safe haven for creativity where staff members are encouraged to question the status quo and think creatively.

3. Encourage cooperation and interdisciplinary teams.

Tear down departmental and team silos and promote cooperation. Collaborating with people who have different backgrounds and skill sets allows for the exchange of ideas and the development of a collaborative culture. Encourage staff members to collaborate on initiatives and projects in order to make use of their combined knowledge and experience.

4. Offer assistance and resources.
Make the technological, tool, and resource investments required to foster innovation. Give staff members the opportunity for training and development so they can improve their abilities and stay current with emerging trends and technologies. Establish a nurturing atmosphere where workers can seek advice and assistance from mentors, coaches, and specialists for their creative projects.

5. Promote a customer-first mentality.
Focus your innovation efforts on the needs and wants of your customers. Encourage staff members to pay close attention to what customers have to say, pinpoint their problems, and create creative solutions to meet their demands. You may develop goods and services that genuinely connect with your clients by learning about their goals and challenges.

11.2.3 Embracing Innovation: Its Benefits
Adopting an innovative culture has many advantages for your company.

1. An edge over competitors
By being innovative, you can set your company apart from the competition and remain on the cutting edge. You may differentiate yourself in the market by creating one-of-a-kind goods,

experiences, and services through constant innovation.

2. Enhanced Productivity and Efficiency
Innovation frequently results in the adoption of new technology and process changes, which can boost productivity and efficiency inside your company. Tasks can be automated and procedures streamlined to free up resources so you can concentrate on value-added work.

3. Better experiences for customers
You can better understand and serve your clients' changing demands when you innovate. You may create unique and unforgettable experiences that thrill your clients and encourage enduring loyalty by coming up with creative ideas.

4. Talent Attraction and Retention: Top talent is drawn to innovative cultures as they look for chances for development and creativity. Talented people who can contribute to the success of your company can be attracted and retained by creating a culture that appreciates and promotes creativity.

5. Flexibility in the Face of Change
Your company will be better equipped to adjust to shifting market conditions and disruptions thanks to innovation. By embracing innovation, you can make sure your company stays robust and relevant by proactively identifying and responding to emerging trends.

In summary

In order to create profitable and long-lasting enterprises, entrepreneurs must embrace an innovative culture. Through the promotion of creativity, adoption of a growth mindset, collaboration, resource and support provision, and a customer-centric approach, entrepreneurs may foster an innovative culture that propels growth, amplifies competitiveness, and generates enduring value. Entrepreneurs can become leaders in their fields and realize their full potential by always looking for fresh concepts, questioning the status quo, and welcoming change.

11.3 Putting Continuous Improvement into Practice

A key component of entrepreneurship is continuous improvement, which enables companies to spur innovation, remain relevant, and adjust to shifting market conditions. This section will discuss the value of putting continuous improvement ideas into practice and how they can support business owners in thriving in a fast-paced, cutthroat industry.

11.3.1 Adopting a Continuous Improvement Culture

In order to execute continuous improvement successfully, entrepreneurs need to cultivate a culture that values development, learning, and innovation. The first step in doing this is to establish a work atmosphere where staff members are encouraged to share their thoughts and recommendations for enhancements. Entrepreneurs may harness the group's creativity and collective expertise by encouraging open communication and teamwork.

Creating frequent feedback loops is one strategy to promote a culture of continuous improvement. Performance reviews, team gatherings, or anonymous suggestion boxes can all be used for this. Through proactive employee feedback gathering, business owners may pinpoint areas in need of enhancement and make the appropriate adjustments.

Additionally, it is critical for entrepreneurs to set a positive example and show that they are dedicated to ongoing development. Entrepreneurs should encourage their team members to pursue learning and development opportunities by adopting a growth mindset and actively seeking them out.

11.3.2 Putting Lean Concepts into Practice

The Toyota Production System is the source of lean concepts, which are well-known for being useful instruments for executing continuous improvement. These guidelines center on reducing waste, boosting productivity, and optimizing value for clients. Entrepreneurs can improve overall business performance and streamline processes by implementing lean principles.

Finding and getting rid of waste is a crucial component of lean principles. This can include things like pointless paperwork, surplus inventory, and ineffective procedures that don't benefit the client. Entrepreneurs may maximize their resources and boost output by locating and getting rid of trash.

The idea of continuous flow is another key component of lean principles. This entails creating procedures that reduce hiccups and bottlenecks to enable a fluid and effective workflow. Entrepreneurs may save lead times, boost customer happiness, and boost overall operational efficiency by putting continuous flow into practice.

11.3.3 Making Use of KPIs (Key Performance Indicators)

KPIs, or key performance indicators, are crucial instruments for gauging and tracking the success of businesses. Entrepreneurs can discover opportunities for development and obtain important insights into the efficacy of their strategy by monitoring pertinent data. KPIs can vary depending on the type of business, but some typical examples are cost per unit, sales income, customer satisfaction, and employee productivity.

It is imperative for entrepreneurs to choose KPIs that are in line with their business goals and objectives when putting them into practice. These measurements must be time-bound, meaningful, quantifiable, attainable, and specific (SMART). Entrepreneurs can drive continuous improvement by identifying trends, seeing possible problems, and making data-driven decisions by defining clear targets and routinely reviewing progress.

11.3.4 Promotion of Innovation and Trials

Continuous improvement has innovation as one of its main drivers. An innovative culture can be developed within an organization by entrepreneurs encouraging their staff members to think outside the box and try out new concepts. Hackathons, creative teams, and brainstorming sessions can all be used to achieve this.

Additionally, entrepreneurs want to foster a risk-free atmosphere where failing is viewed as a chance for improvement. Entrepreneurs can enable their team members to experiment and come up with creative ideas by adopting a mindset that promotes taking measured risks.

Additionally, technology can be used by

entrepreneurs to support innovation and ongoing development. Entrepreneurs may speed up innovation and promote continuous improvement by making investments in technologies and systems that facilitate teamwork, idea sharing, and quick prototyping.

11.3.5 Ongoing Education and Training

Maintaining a commitment to lifelong learning and growth is necessary for continuous improvement. It is advisable for entrepreneurs to motivate their associates to explore avenues for professional growth, such as participating in online courses, conferences, or workshops. Entrepreneurs can improve the skills and knowledge of their workforce by investing in their growth and development. This, in turn, helps to improve the business as a whole.

Entrepreneurs should also be abreast of developments in the market, upcoming technologies, and industry trends. Entrepreneurs who keep themselves educated are better able to recognize possibilities for improvement early on and modify their plans of action accordingly.

11.3.6 Putting Feedback Loops in Place

Feedback loops are necessary for ongoing development. Entrepreneurs ought to set up procedures for getting input from stakeholders, including staff members and clients. Surveys, focus groups, and social media listening can all be used for this. Entrepreneurs may identify opportunities for improvement, learn a great deal about the requirements and preferences of their customers, and make well-informed decisions to promote continual improvement by aggressively soliciting feedback.

Additionally, business owners ought to foster a constructive criticism culture within their company. Entrepreneurs can promote a culture of ongoing learning and development by giving regular feedback to staff members and encouraging them to give feedback to one another.

11.3.7 Honoring Achievements and Celebrating Success

A crucial component of putting continuous improvement into practice is recognizing and applauding accomplishments. Owners ought to thank staff members for their contributions to the company's success. Rewards, like bonuses or other forms of compensation, can be used to achieve this. Entrepreneurs may inspire team members and uphold a culture of continuous improvement by recognizing and applauding accomplishments.

To sum up, continuous development is essential for the success of an entrepreneur. Entrepreneurs can drive innovation, adapt to change, and stay ahead in a dynamic and competitive business landscape by embracing a culture of continuous improvement, putting lean principles into practice, using KPIs, encouraging innovation and experimentation, promoting continuous learning and development, putting feedback loops in place, and celebrating success.

11.4 Recognizing and Addressing Industry Upheavals

In the ever-evolving business environment of today, entrepreneurs must be able to foresee and react to disruptions in their industry, in addition to being able to adjust to change. Disruptions can take many different forms, including changes in customer behavior, new competitors entering the market, governmental changes, and technical breakthroughs. In order to remain ahead of the curve and preserve a competitive advantage, entrepreneurs need to be proactive in spotting possible disruptions and creating plans to deal with them.

11.4.1 Recognizing Possible Interruptions

Finding possible disruptors is the first step in foreseeing and responding to disruptions in the sector. This necessitates a thorough comprehension of market trends, your sector, and the variables that could affect your company. Keep up with changes in customer preferences, the competitive landscape, and technology improvements. To spot new trends and possible disruptors, do routine market research and analysis.

Interacting with your stakeholders and consumers is one efficient method to spot possible disruptions. Pay attention to their opinions, be aware of their problems, and predict their needs going forward. Maintaining a relationship with your target market can help you identify any impending disruptions and make the necessary adjustments to your organization.

11.4.2 Adopting an Innovative Culture
Developing an innovative culture inside your company is crucial to being able to react to market upheavals. Urge the members of your team to question the status quo, think outside the box, and investigate novel concepts. Establish a setting that values experimentation and measures risk-taking.

To keep up with the latest developments in technology and business trends, make research and development investments. Work together with outside partners to access cutting-edge innovations and benefit from their experience, such as startups, research institutes, or universities. You may put your company in a position to proactively respond to disruptions and grab new possibilities by adopting an innovative culture.

11.4.3 Putting Continuous Improvement into Practice

Establishing a culture of continuous improvement is essential not just for encouraging innovation but also for anticipating and responding to upheavals in the business. Motivate your staff to review and improve your company's procedures, goods, and services on a regular basis. Evaluate your operations on a regular basis to find areas for improvement and make the necessary adjustments to improve efficacy and efficiency.

Accept criticism from clients, staff members, and other stakeholders in order to learn about possible areas for development. Use data analytics to find trends, patterns, and areas that could be optimized. You may maintain your agility and put yourself in a better position to handle disruptions by making constant improvements to your company.

11.4.4 Formulating a Plan for Handling Disruptions

Upon identification of possible disruptions, it is imperative to formulate a complete reaction strategy. This plan should describe how your company will adjust to changes and grow during that period. While formulating your reaction plan, take into account the following steps:

Analyze the possible effects: Determine how each disruption might affect your company. Determine the opportunities and hazards connected to each disruption, then rank them according to the possible impact.

Planning for scenarios: Create a variety of scenarios according to the possible interruptions and their effects. Think about the most likely, worst-case, and best-case situations. This will assist you in planning for a variety of scenarios and creating tactics that are suitable for each one.

Diversify your offerings: To lessen the effects of disruptions, think about extending your range of products and services. Investigate untapped markets, create novel products, or enter adjacent markets. You can lessen your reliance on a particular product or market and strengthen your resistance to disruptions by broadening your offers.

Form strategic alliances: Work together with other companies or industry participants to cooperatively navigate disruptions. Forming strategic alliances can give you access to new markets, resources, or technology that will enable you to respond to disruptions more skillfully.

Invest in technology. Use it to streamline business processes and fend off disruptions. Utilize data analytics, automation, artificial intelligence, and other cutting-edge technology to boost productivity, make better decisions, and spot new opportunities.

Continue to be flexible and agile. Foster an environment of flexibility and agility within your company. Motivate your group to welcome change, be receptive to fresh perspectives, and react fast to changes in the market. You can take advantage of fresh opportunities and navigate disruptions more skillfully if you remain flexible and agile.

Evaluate and monitor: Keep an eye on the market, industry developments, and the success of your response plans. Assess your reaction tactics on a regular basis and tweak them as necessary. Remain alert and ready to change course if needed.

In the face of industry changes, you can position your company to not just survive but prosper by creating a thorough reaction plan and taking proactive steps. To stay ahead of the curve and make a lasting impression on your sector, embrace change, encourage innovation, and constantly improve your firm.

SUSTAINING SUCCESS AND LEAVING A LEGACY

12.1 Sustaining Enterprise Long-Term Performance

Best wishes! You've established a prosperous corporate empire. However, the adventure is far from over. Long-term success demands consistent work, flexibility, and a calculated strategy. We'll look at the primary elements in this section that go into keeping your company successful and creating a lasting legacy.

12.1.1 Fostering an Excellence Culture

Developing an excellent culture inside your company is essential to sustaining long-term success. Setting high expectations and standards for your team members is the first step in doing this. Promote a culture of innovation and constant development where all employees are dedicated to providing outstanding goods and services.

Give your staff members the tools, instructions, and encouragement they need to succeed in their positions if you want to cultivate an excellence-focused culture. Provide chances for professional development and progress, and acknowledge and honor exceptional achievement. Investing in your team helps them become more skilled and capable while also encouraging loyalty and a sense of dedication to the company.

12.1.2 Developing Client Connections

Building great relationships with your clients

is essential to long-term success, as they are the lifeblood of your organization. Always seek to comprehend how their requirements and preferences are changing, and then modify your offerings to meet those needs. Utilize social media, feedback sessions, and surveys to regularly interact with your clients in order to learn more about their expectations.

Go above and beyond to exceed your customers' expectations in order to deliver great customer service. Address any problems or issues as soon as possible and efficiently, and make it a point to provide a unique and unforgettable experience every time. By establishing trusting bonds with your clients, you can encourage their loyalty and win over important brand ambassadors who will promote your company favorably.

12.1.3 Accepting Adaptation and Innovation
Maintaining an advantage in a corporate environment that is changing quickly requires innovation and adaptability. To find chances for innovation, keep an eye on market trends, technological developments, and consumer preferences. Promote an innovative and creative culture in your company where fresh concepts are embraced and put to the test.

Adopt an attitude of continuous improvement and look for opportunities to improve your processes, services, and goods on a regular basis. Urge the members of your team to question the status quo and think creatively. You can maintain an advantage over your competitors and secure the long-term viability of your company by welcoming innovation and adaptability.

12.1.4 Setting Objectives and Strategic Planning
Setting goals and engaging in strategic planning are necessary to sustain long-term success. Review and revise your company plan on a regular basis to keep it current with shifting goals and market conditions. Establish attainable, quantifiable, and well-defined goals for your company and divide them into manageable chunks.

Create a future plan that outlines the tactics and steps needed to realize your long-term goals. Monitor and assess your development on a regular basis, and make any required corrections. Establishing strategic objectives and monitoring your progress on a regular basis will help you keep your company headed toward long-term success.

12.1.5 Developing a Business Plan with Resilience
Building a robust company model that can endure obstacles and uncertainty is crucial to long-term success. To lessen reliance on a single source, diversify your consumer base and revenue sources. Keep an eye on and evaluate your financial performance on a constant basis. Recognize possible dangers and take proactive steps to reduce them.

In order to stay ahead of market trends and foresee potential disruptions, invest in research and development. Establish trusting bonds with partners, suppliers, and other stakeholders to establish a network of cooperation. You may successfully navigate through difficult times and secure the long-term prosperity of your empire by developing a robust business plan.

12.1.6 Making a Social Impact and Giving Back
Making a positive social impact and giving back to society are essential for successful entrepreneurs. Think about including CSR (corporate social responsibility) programs in your business plan. Encourage causes that share your goals and beliefs by volunteering, making philanthropic contributions, or adopting sustainable corporate practices.

Giving back to the community benefits society as a whole, improves the reputation of your business, and draws in socially conscious clients. Having a positive social influence can be a potent way to alter the world for the better and leave a lasting legacy.

12.1.7 Making Plans for Succession and Exit Strategies
Even if it seems too soon to consider closing your firm when you have recently found success, future planning is crucial. Create a thorough exit strategy that details your choices for leaving the company, including mergers, sales, and succession planning.

If you want to guarantee a seamless transfer of leadership inside your company, think about identifying and nurturing future leaders. Keep records of important systems, procedures, and expertise to make the transfer of duties easier. You can secure your company's future and leave a lasting legacy by making plans for succession and exit options.

In summary, sustaining long-term corporate success necessitates a comprehensive and strategic approach. Establish a culture of excellence, foster relationships with customers, welcome innovation, and adjust to shifting market conditions. Establish strategic objectives, create a robust business plan, and contribute to the community. Lastly, think ahead by organizing your succession and exit options. You can maintain the success of your company and leave a lasting legacy by adhering to these rules.

12.2 Business Continuity Planning

It is imperative that you, as an entrepreneur, make plans for your company's long-term viability and continuation. Although achieving success is the ultimate goal, being ready for unforeseen events and potential obstacles that may come along the way is just as vital. Creating a thorough business continuity plan can help you make sure your company can bounce back quickly and easily from setbacks.

12.2.1 Recognizing Possible Dangers and Weaknesses

The first step in creating a business continuity strategy is to determine the risks and weaknesses that can affect your company. These risks can take many different forms, including natural disasters, economic downturns, technological malfunctions, and even modifications to laws and regulations. Determine which aspects of your company's activities are most vulnerable to these threats by conducting a thorough assessment.

Take into account your company's location and the possibility of natural disasters in the surrounding area. Analyze your supply chain's stability and the possible effects of any interruptions. Evaluate your IT infrastructure's susceptibility and the possible repercussions of a cyberattack or data leak. By being aware of these dangers, you may create plans to lessen their effects and guarantee your company's survival.

12.2.2 Creating a Plan for Business Continuity

Upon identifying the possible risks and weaknesses, the next step is to create a business continuity strategy. The actions and protocols to be taken in the case of an interruption or emergency should be described in this plan. It ought to offer a road map for how your company will carry on and take care of its clients amid trying times.

Establishing a crisis management team to oversee the business continuity plan's implementation should be the first step. Important staff members from several areas who possess the skills and information necessary to make important choices should be on this team. To guarantee a coordinated reaction, give each team member a clear job and set of tasks.

Next, describe the steps that need to be taken in case of an interruption. This could include contingency plans for your technological systems' backup and recovery, a list of other vendors or suppliers you can depend on in case the supply chain is disrupted, and communication guidelines for informing your stakeholders, customers, and staff.

Furthermore, think about the financial effects of a disruption and create plans to handle cash flow in trying circumstances. This could entail setting up emergency savings or looking into insurance alternatives to lessen possible monetary losses.

12.2.3 Business Continuity Plan Testing and Updates

Creating a business continuity plan requires ongoing effort. To make sure the plan is effective, it is essential to test and update it frequently. Regularly carrying out exercises and simulations will enable you to spot any holes or weak points in the strategy and make the necessary corrections.

Engage your crisis management team in these drills and assess how well they executed the strategy. In addition to offering a chance to train and enlighten team members on their duties and responsibilities, this will assist in identifying areas that require development.

Furthermore, keep up with the most recent advancements and trends in your sector and consider how they can affect your business continuity plan. It's critical to modify your plan when new hazards arise and technology advances.

12.2.4 Building Connections with Important Stakeholders
Having solid ties with important stakeholders can be quite helpful during times of crisis. Maintaining open channels of communication and fostering a sense of trust among your staff, clients, vendors, and investors will help guarantee their collaboration and support when things get tough.

Educate your staff on the business continuity strategy and their responsibilities for carrying it out. Promote candid communication and provide them with the tools and instructions they need to deal with interruptions in a professional manner.

Keep in constant contact with your suppliers and customers to let them know about any impending interruptions and the measures you are taking to lessen their effects. Even in trying times, you may preserve solid relationships and establish trust by acting with initiative and honesty in your communication.

12.2.5 Getting Help and Advice from Professionals
Creating a business continuity plan can be difficult, particularly for small companies with little funding. Think about consulting with professionals that specialize in business continuity planning for guidance and support.

Seeking advice and valuable insights from experts in risk management and business continuity is highly recommended. They may assist you in identifying possible hazards, creating winning strategies, and making sure your strategy complies with accepted industry standards.

In addition, think about becoming a member of networking or industry associations that concentrate on catastrophe recovery and business continuity. Through these networks, you can have access to tools, best practices, and encouragement from other business owners who have encountered comparable difficulties.

In summary
Making plans for business continuity is a crucial

part of being an entrepreneur. You may guarantee the long-term viability and profitability of your company by recognizing possible risks, creating a thorough plan, testing and updating it frequently, and building trusting connections with important stakeholders. Remember that what distinguishes great entrepreneurs is their capacity for adaptation and problem-solving. Accept the responsibility of creating a business continuity plan and set yourself up for future expansion and prosperity.

12.3 Giving Back and Having an Influence on Society

In addition to concentrating on growing a profitable company, entrepreneurs should also consider contributing to the community and having a beneficial social influence. We will look at the different ways that entrepreneurs may leave a lasting legacy and give back to their communities in this chapter.

12.3.1 The Value of Corporate Social Responsibility

The concept of social responsibility holds that companies have a duty to behave in a way that is advantageous to society at large. It includes a company's ethical, environmental, and social effects in addition to just producing a profit. Entrepreneurs who embrace social responsibility not only improve their brand and draw in a socially conscious clientele, but they may also truly change the world.

12.3.2 How to Include Social Impact in Your Business Plan

Including social impact from the outset of your business strategy is one of the best methods to achieve it. There are several ways to accomplish this, including:

12.3.2.1 Socially Aware Goods and Services

Think about creating goods or services that deal with environmental or social concerns. For instance, you may design a technology solution that increases educational access in marginalized regions or launch a sustainable fashion line using materials produced ethically. You can attract clients who share your values and effect positive change by associating your company with a social cause.

12.3.2.2 Programs for Corporate Social Responsibility

Employees and the community can greatly benefit from the implementation of corporate social responsibility (CSR) programs within your company. These programs may involve philanthropic donations, volunteer work, or collaborations with nonprofit groups. You can cultivate a positive work culture and give your employees a sense of purpose by encouraging them to participate in social causes.

12.3.2.3 Supply Chains with Social Responsibility

Make sure your supply chain is in line with your objectives for social impact by evaluating it. Think about collaborating with vendors who place a high value on ethical sourcing, sustainable environmental practices, and fair labor standards. You can help create a more just and sustainable global economy by encouraging ethical behavior across your whole supply chain.

12.3.3 Charitable Giving and Philanthropy

Giving to charities and philanthropy are effective approaches for business owners to change society. You can make a long-lasting difference and support organizations that are important to you by setting up a foundation or contributing a portion of your revenues. Take into account causes that are consistent with your beliefs and have a significant effect on the community when deciding which organizations to support.

12.3.4 Assisting and Guiding Fellow Entrepreneurs

Aspiring entrepreneurs might benefit from your knowledge and experience as another way to give back. Think about taking part in entrepreneurship initiatives that assist marginalized populations or becoming a mentor. You can help others overcome obstacles and realize their entrepreneurial aspirations by offering advice and encouragement.

12.3.5 Sustainability of the Environment

Entrepreneurs can have a positive social and environmental impact in addition. Think about introducing eco-friendly procedures in your company, such as cutting back on trash, employing sustainable materials, and saving energy. Making sustainability a top priority will help you reduce your environmental impact and encourage others to follow suit.

12.3.6 Social Impact Measurement and Reporting

It is critical to track and report on the results of your social impact initiatives to make sure they are successful. This can be accomplished using a variety of measures, including the quantity of lives impacted, environmental benefits realized, or money raised. You can pinpoint areas for development and let stakeholders know how you're making an impact by keeping track of your progress.

12.3.7 Working with Other Socially Responsible Companies

You may increase the impact of your social impact initiatives by collaborating with other ethically-minded companies. Think about joining forces with groups that share your values to take on more significant social concerns or take part in group projects. By working together, you may take advantage of one another's advantages and have an influence that is more profound and long-lasting.

12.3.8 Getting Workers Interested in Social Impact
Getting your staff involved in social impact projects can improve job satisfaction and give them a sense of purpose. Motivate them to donate their time, take part in fundraising activities, or lend a hand with humanitarian concerns. Establishing a socially conscious culture in your company will help you draw in and keep top individuals who are driven to change the world.

12.3.9 Establishing a Durable Legacy
It is crucial for entrepreneurs to consider the long-term effects of their ventures in addition to their immediate financial gains. Think about how you can leave a lasting legacy by starting foundations, initiatives, or scholarships that will carry on with their societal influence long after you are gone. You can make sure that your business journey leaves a lasting and beneficial impact on the world by making plans for the future.

In conclusion, a key component of being a successful entrepreneur is contributing to society and having an impact on it. You can leave a lasting legacy that extends beyond financial success by integrating social responsibility into your business strategy, practicing charity, mentoring others, and advocating for environmental sustainability. Seize the chance to use your entrepreneurial path to change the world and leave a positive legacy.

12.4 Getting Ready for Succession Planning and Exit Strategies

It's critical for entrepreneurs to plan for the future in addition to concentrating on developing and expanding their companies. Making arrangements for succession planning and exit strategies is an essential part of this strategy. Though it might seem strange to consider quitting your company when you are just getting started, having a well-thought-out exit strategy can actually help ensure the sustainability and long-term success of your endeavor.

12.4.1 Comprehending Exit Strategies

An exit strategy is a plan that outlines how you intend to ultimately quit your company. Taking preemptive measures to guarantee that you can leave your company on your terms—selling it, transferring ownership to a family member or employee, or even going public with an IPO—is important. A well-thought-out exit strategy will optimize your company's worth and facilitate a seamless handoff.

There are a few typical exit tactics that business owners think about:

12.4.1.1 Selling the Company
Selling your company is among the most popular ways to leave the workforce. This entails locating a buyer who is prepared to purchase your company and assume management of its activities. You can go on to new endeavors or enjoy retirement by selling your business and receiving a sizable financial return. It's critical to get your company ready for sale by making sure it has a clear value proposition, correct financial records, and appeals to prospective purchasers.

12.4.1.2 Giving the Company to Family or Workers
Transferring ownership of your company to a family member or employee is another departure plan. If you have a capable and eager successor who wants to take over the company, this can be a terrific alternative. It enables you to uphold a heritage and guarantee that your company prospers under new management. To guarantee a smooth transition, it is crucial to give due consideration to the successor's abilities and dedication and to provide them with the required guidance and assistance.

12.4.1.3 Public Offering (IPO)

The ideal exit plan for certain business owners is to go public with their company through an initial public offering (IPO). Through the sale of company shares to the general public, you can raise a substantial amount of money and give your current shareholders liquidity. The process of going public can be difficult and time-consuming, involving investment banks and legal counsel in addition to regulatory compliance. When considering this exit plan, it is crucial to thoroughly assess the viability and possible advantages of an initial public offering (IPO).

12.4.2 The Significance of Succession Management

The process of identifying and grooming future leaders inside your company to guarantee a seamless transfer of leadership is known as succession planning. It is essential to the long-term viability of your company since it makes sure that it can run efficiently without you. Identification of important positions within your company, evaluation of prospective successors' qualifications, and provision of appropriate training and growth opportunities are all part of succession planning.

12.4.2.1 Guaranteeing Persistence

Maintaining continuity in your company's operations is one of the key goals of succession planning. When the time comes for you to stand down, you may make sure that there is a seamless transfer of leadership by identifying and training possible successors. This reduces interruptions and enables your company to go on efficiently even in the event of unforeseen circumstances like retirement or illness.

12.4.2.2 Preserving institutional information

Another benefit of succession planning is that it keeps institutional knowledge inside your company. Being an entrepreneur means that you have probably gained a lot of information and expertise that will help your company succeed. You may transfer this knowledge and guarantee its preservation inside your business by identifying and training future successors. This is advantageous for your company's overall growth and sustainability, as well as for the next generation of leaders.

12.4.2.3 Creating Leaders of the Future

You have a chance to nurture future leaders in your company through succession planning. You may prepare people for leadership roles by recognizing those who have great potential and giving them the training and development opportunities they need. Long-term business benefits aside, this also improves staff retention and engagement. Workers are more likely to be driven and dedicated to the company's success if they perceive a clear path for advancement.

12.4.3 Procedures for Succession Planning and

Exit Strategies

Take into account the following actions as you get ready for succession planning and exit strategies:

12.4.3.1 Evaluating Your Choices

Examine your possibilities for departure tactics first. Examine the benefits and drawbacks of each choice to determine which best suits your long-term objectives and company vision.

12.4.3.2 Finding Probable Successors

If you are thinking of transferring ownership of your company to a relative or an employee, find possible heirs within your company. Seek out candidates who exhibit leadership potential, comprehend your industry well, and share your values and vision.

12.4.3.3 Formulating Plans for Succession

After identifying possible heirs, create succession plans for every important position in your company. These plans ought to contain a development plan for each successor in addition to outlining the procedures and deadlines required for leadership transitions.

12.4.3.4 Sharing and Putting the Plans into Action

Share your succession plans and departure strategy with important parties, including family members, investors, and staff. Make sure everyone knows what the plans are and what their roles and duties are during the transition. Carry out the plans in a methodical and well-organized way, offering the resources and assistance required to ensure a seamless transition.

12.4.3.5 Observing and Modifying

Keep a close eye on the development of your succession and exit strategies and change as necessary. Your plans might need to be revised as your company grows and situations alter in order for them to stay effective.

In summary

Being a successful entrepreneur requires preparing for exit plans and succession planning. A well-planned exit strategy can help you optimize your company's worth and guarantee a seamless handoff when the time comes. Similar to this, succession planning enables you to secure the long-term viability of your company and cultivate future leaders within your organization. You will be able to leave a lasting legacy and plan for the future with effectiveness if you follow the instructions in this chapter.